# EDGAR ALLAN POE

## Genius in Torment

**EDGAR ALLAN POE**

# EDGAR ALLAN POE

**Genius in Torment**

# William Jay Jacobs

McGraw-Hill Book Company
New York   St. Louis   San Francisco   Auckland
Düsseldorf   Johannesburg   Kuala Lumpur
London   Mexico   Montreal   New Delhi
Panama   Paris   São Paulo   Singapore   Sydney
Tokyo   Toronto

To the teachers of
Avondale School, Cincinnati, Ohio (1938–1947),
this book is gratefully dedicated.

Library of Congress Cataloging in Publication Data

Jacobs, William Jay.
    Edgar Allan Poe:   genius in torment.

    (American writers)
    Bibliography:   p.
    Includes index.
    SUMMARY:  A biography of the troubled nineteenth-
century author with a discussion of his prose and poetry
which greatly influenced prominent artists and writers
throughout the world.
    1. Poe, Edgar Allan, 1809–1849—Juvenile literature.
[1. Poe, Edgar Allan, 1809–1849.   2. Authors, American]
I. Title.
PS2631.J34        818'.3'09 [B] [92]        74-32010
ISBN 0-07-032158-2 lib. bdg.

1234567MUBP7898765

# contents

# introduction

It was Wednesday afternoon, October 3, 1849. Rain, light but insistent, fell on the streets of Baltimore. As Joseph Walker, a typesetter for the *Baltimore Sun,* made his way along busy Lombard Street, an unusual sight caught his eye. He stopped short and looked closely.

Outside of Gunner's Hall, a popular saloon of the day, a man lay sprawled on his back. He was clothed in a torn black suit coat and a pair of baggy gray trousers, clearly several sizes too large for him. Because of the rain everything he wore was soaking wet.

Such a sight ordinarily might not have surprised Walker. It was election day in Baltimore, and in the democratic spirit of the post-Jacksonian era, political parties unashamedly competed with each other to harness chronic drunks, who then would be transported to different polling places in the city. At each location they would cast a vote. The reward for such chicanery was a drink, or perhaps even a whole bottle.

But as Joseph Walker instantly surmised, the

limp form on the sidewalk was not the usual drunk, sleeping off an evening's tippling. For although half unconscious, the apparent derelict grasped firmly in his hand an expensive, elegantly worked Malacca cane.

For a moment Walker hesitated. Then, advancing closer, he knelt beside the prostrate figure. The face he saw was a translucent white, drained almost entirely of natural color. Somehow, out of his stupor, the helpless victim managed to identify himself. "Poe" was his name—Edgar Allan Poe. And would Walker please call the doctor who knew about his case, Dr. J. E. Snodgrass?

Hastily, Walker scribbled a note to Dr. Snodgrass, describing the desperately ill Poe as a "gentleman, rather the worse for wear . . . in need of immediate assistance."

Snodgrass, responding immediately to the message, rushed to the tavern. He had treated Poe before and was aware that his patient was one of America's best known literary figures: a poet, story-teller, and critic—but also an erratic, tempestuous personality. Nor was this the first time he had become ill from too much drink. Snodgrass was an experienced physician. But he had not practiced medicine for many years, having turned to a career in literature. A temperance advocate, he was familiar with the symptoms of acute alcoholism—and it was in connection with that illness that he had met Poe many years before. Yet Poe's present condition puzzled him; he suspected that his patient was not suffering from a typical drunken hangover to be "slept off" overnight. This was different —and far more serious.

Soon the horse-drawn ambulance summoned by Dr. Snodgrass was careening dangerously through the unpaved streets of Baltimore, racing to the hospital. There, nurses cut Poe's rain-drenched clothing from his body and bundled him in sheets and blankets. Too exhausted to speak, the poet lay motionless through most of the night. Then toward morning he began to tremble until his every bone shook violently. He talked without letup, angrily raging at shadows on the walls. A cold sweat broke out over his entire body.

Poe ranted on deliriously for three days. "Reynolds! Reynolds!" he would cry, to the puzzlement of the attendants hovering at his bedside. Nurses had to restrain him to keep him in bed. At three o'clock on Sunday morning, October 7, Poe's condition took an unexpected turn. Thoroughly spent from his great mental agony, he sank back on his pillows. Then after gently sighing, "Lord help my poor soul," he fell asleep. Two hours later he died.

The cause of Poe's death, like so much in his brief life—he was forty when he died—remains shrouded in mystery. But now, a century and a quarter after his tragic end, we know more about him. And no wonder. With the possible exception

3

of Walt Whitman, more has been written about Poe than about any other American author. Yet despite an outpouring of detailed critical and biographical studies, controversy still rages about his character and the quality of his work. While he lived Poe's enemies portrayed him as a sadistic fiend, petty, dishonest, and hopelessly addicted to drugs. And even today his writing arouses among some critics a reaction of utter disgust; they regard his output as little more than sickly sentimentalism, a mixture of low-level inventiveness and morbid claptrap. Henry James despised him.

Poe's admirers are equally partisan. Thomas Hardy regarded him as "the first to realize to the full the possibility of the English language in thought and rhyme." James Russell Lowell considered him "the only fearless American critic." To Baudelaire he was almost literally a saint to whom prayers could be addressed. W. H. Auden viewed some of his poems as among the finest ever produced by an American, citing particularly "To Helen" and "The City in the Sea." "The Bells" and "The Raven"—whatever their literary quality—are two of the best known poems in the English language. More than any other single writer, Poe was personally responsible for inventing the detective story and the science fiction tale. He set a standard for the construction of the short story. And few if any have ever equaled his ability to evoke and sustain a mood of horror.

For high school and college youth in today's turbulent, contradictory times, Poe has exercised a magnetic appeal. Young people appear to identify with him. Conflict and contradiction, after all, were underlying themes of his life. A melancholy dreamer, he was forced to cope with the reality of what he sensed to be an uncaring, or perhaps even a conspiratorial, universe. The product of good schools, reared for the life of a gentleman in an atmosphere of gentility, restraint, and refinement, he emerged a loner—luckless, bitter, quarrelsome, alienated.

In his works he created a grotesque, terrifying, fantasy world. Even the passage of many years does not erase from one's memory his psychedelic visions of flashing, luminous colors or his chilling portraits of burial before death. These products of Poe's imagination, no less than the wreck that he made of his personal life, are topics of perennial fascination. Nor is he a stranger to our own era in his attempts to cope with psychological crisis, or to achieve heightened artistic consciousness through the use of drugs.

Because of his relevance, Poe—that strange, disquieting figure from our past—deserves to be examined again now. This is so, even if a full understanding of his harrowing existence continues to elude us.

# 1

## *childhood at home and abroad* (1809–1820)

The year 1809 was largely uneventful in America's history. In that year James Madison was inaugurated as the nation's fourth president, extending the Virginia dynasty of chief executives begun by George Washington and which remained, except for one four-year period, unbroken until 1825. Already the nightmare of the Founding Fathers— strife among competing factions—had reared its head. Federalists contended with Republicans, rich with poor, and commercial-industrial Northerners with agrarian, slave-holding Southerners. The experiment of constitutional government was by no means secure; and in Great Britain, when the ministers of King George could spare a moment's thought from the stomach-churning threat of Napoleon, they still pondered ways to regain Britain's lost American colonies.

Thin lines of American pioneers meanwhile had begun to thread their way through the passes of the Appalachian mountains and then along the westward-flowing rivers to sparsely populated settlements on the frontier. But the center of civilized life in America was still along the narrow band of the eastern seaboard, particularly in the thriving port cities of Charleston, Philadelphia, New York, and Boston.

It was in Boston on January 19, 1809, that a son, Edgar, was born to David and Elizabeth Poe. Both parents were professional actors. Elizabeth Poe was herself the daughter of an actress, Elizabeth ("Betty") Arnold, who had come to America from England hoping for greater success on the stage. Elizabeth, the daughter, made her acting debut in America at the age of nine. By fourteen she was already playing leading parts in Shakespearean drama. Living in the close companionship dictated by theater life, she married a fellow player, Charles Hopkins, when she was only fifteen. The marriage ended in October 1805 when Hopkins died, probably of the plague. At the age of eighteen Elizabeth Arnold Hopkins was a widow. Her own mother had died when she was eleven.

Six months later the young widow married David Poe, twenty-one, a former law student who had forsaken his books for the excitement of a career on the stage. David's father had been a quartermaster in George Washington's armies during the Revolutionary War. A loyal supporter of the Colonial cause, he loaned the government forty thousand dollars of his own money and came to be know affectionately as "General Poe." Lafayette, the French hero of America's struggle for freedom, spoke with gratitude of the food and clothing that Poe supplied the Continental Army; on a nostalgic visit to America in 1824, he kissed the ground above the grave of his dead comrade in arms.

Poe's loans, however, were never repaid, and after his death his wife and seven children, of whom David was the oldest, were forced to live in a state of near poverty. Young David's only means of support was the meager income he gleaned from minor theatrical roles.

Two sons were born to David and Elizabeth Poe: William Henry Leonard in 1807 and Edgar in 1809. By necessity Elizabeth was back on the Boston stage singing and dancing just three weeks after Edgar's birth. With an extra mouth to feed, the first son, "Henry," was soon sent to live with David's family in Baltimore. Elizabeth's fine acting, especially in her Shakespearean parts such as Ophelia in *Hamlet,* won high praise from critics. But David Poe's notices grew steadily worse. One critic offhandedly dismissed his performance, noting that Poe was "Poo." Before long he could not get parts. The family's financial plight became desperate.

In July 1810, David Poe unexplainably left his family. To this day it is not certain what happened. Most scholars argue that David, a weak person discouraged by his failure in the theater, deserted Elizabeth and young Edgar. Others believe that he returned to his home in Baltimore to care for his other son, Henry. There was correspondence between Elizabeth and David Poe, some of it dating after July 1810. But Elizabeth directed that on her death the letters should be burned. Her instructions were followed, and the mystery remains unsolved.

Whatever the truth, David Poe was gone, and Elizabeth was left alone to care for herself and Edgar. To compound the tragedy, five months later she gave birth to another child, Rosalie.

Clutching at any straw to make a living, Elizabeth Poe joined a company of traveling players based in Richmond, Virginia. But under the strain of frequent performances and unceasing travel her already frail health declined. Weakened by tuberculosis, the most common fatal disease of the day, she was confined to her bed, every day sinking closer to death.

Her tragic case received wide coverage in the Richmond newspapers and inspired a generous outpouring of charitable contributions. Women of the town who admired her work on stage brought pastries and sweets to cheer her. Little Edgar, then an intelligent and sensitive three-year-old, must have wondered why his mother no longer took him to see her perform on stage. Instead she remained in bed. Sometimes she coughed and moaned. The memory of his mother wasting away with disease would long continue to haunt Edgar's mind.

On December 8, 1811, at the age of twenty-four, Elizabeth Poe died.

Knowing that the end was near she had arranged for Rosalie to be housed for a time with one of the kindly local ladies who had given her aid and sympathy, Mrs. William Mackenzie. Edgar was to live in the household of Mrs. John Allan and her prosperous merchant husband.

As Mrs. Allan carried Edgar out of the dingy room in the boardinghouse where his mother had died, she lifted the boy for one more look at her body. The burial was in Old St. John's Church-yard—not in the sacred ground of the church, but in an area away from the other coffins, near the cemetery wall. Regardless of the popular acclaim heaped on actors and actresses in early nine-teenth-century America, the theatrical profession was not considered respectable. Its practitioners were generally thought of as immoral. Thus the grave of the talented Elizabeth Poe remained unmarked by any monument until 1928.

That young Edgar missed his mother's love there can be no doubt. Yet certainly he found himself in improved surroundings with the Allans. John Allan was a rising merchant, active in the tobacco trade but ambitiously expanding his deal-ings in cloth, grain, hardware, and slaves.

Born in Scotland, Allan had been orphaned at an early age. He was both by personality and circumstance a practical man of affairs, inclined to devote most of his attention to the hard realities of life. Although not without a sense of humor, he took particular pride in having complete command of his emotions.

John Allan's wife, Frances, was of a strikingly different temperament. Childless after eight years of marriage, she first persuaded her reluctant husband to take little Edgar Poe into the Allan household; then she proceeded to shower the precocious curly-headed child with tender affection. Her sister, Anne Moore Valentine, lived with the Allans in their quarters above "Ellis and Allan, General Merchants" on Richmond's Capitol Square. After some hesitation she, too, grew fond of the likeable Poe orphan.

For his part, Edgar was swept up in a whole new world. There were visits to elegant plantations in the country, new playmates, fine clothes, and as much good food as he could eat. Pushed to the recesses of his mind were the dark, ill-smelling boardinghouses which were all he had known traveling from city to city with his theatrical parents.

Before long John Allan gave in to his wife's pleading and agreed to take Edgar into the family as a foster child. From that point the boy became known as Edgar Allan Poe. But Allan, a cautious

Scotsman, did not go so far as to adopt his charge legally. Legal adoption was not a common practice at the time. More importantly, Allan was the prospective heir to a large fortune. Only thirty-one years old when he sheltered Edgar, he probably still hoped for children of his own—a hope not without basis from his experience, since he already had one illegitimate son in Richmond. If formally adopted, Edgar would have become a principal heir in line for the money which Allan expected to pass on. The canny merchant was prepared to "bide a wee bit" before making such an irrevocable decision.

Meanwhile, Allan took care to give Edgar the finest education money could buy. He enrolled the boy first in a traditional "dame school," something like a modern kindergarten operated by a neighborhood lady. Next, for about a year Edgar attended a school run by Master William Ewing. He was a bright, happy student, by now very much coddled by his "Mama," as he called Frances Allan; and sternly but judiciously guided by John Allan, or "Pa," as young Poe called the man who already was exerting a dominant influence on his young life.

The year 1815 saw the final defeat of Napoleon at Waterloo. It witnessed, too, the Treaty of Ghent, bringing peace between Great Britain and the United States in the War of 1812. After the prolonged wars growing out of the French Revolution, Europe could at last breathe easily. The sea lanes, closed for years by naval battles and blockades, were again open to commerce. Eagerly, merchants in America and Europe prepared for a bonanza of new trade.

John Allan and his business partner, Charles Ellis, calculated that an overseas branch of Ellis and Allan, based in England, would almost certainly return handsome profits. On June 23, 1815, Allan sailed for Liverpool accompanied by his wife, Frances, her sister Anne Valentine ("Aunt Nancy" to Edgar), and six-year-old Edgar.

Especially for Edgar, the month-long journey aboard the *Lothair* was an occasion of high adventure. With eager curiosity he explored the ship, asked endless questions of the sailors, and—already an avid reader—spent hours at the side of "Mama" poring over storybooks.

At Liverpool there were exciting new sights to see: old churches, colorful military ceremonies, children playing strange games. But for a boy as thoroughly Southern in his upbringing as Edgar, there was one element missing—there were no blacks. Some of Poe's earliest memories were of sunny days and long evenings spent among Negroes in Richmond's slave quarters, listening to their deeply moving songs and stories, absorbing the cadence and hypnotic rhythm of their voices. The influence of these contacts with Negro culture is evident in the style and content of Poe's writing.

But if the sensitive youngster was perplexed by the absence of blacks in Great Britain, he was soon completely absorbed in the moods of his new surroundings. Edgar later remembered vividly the rains and mists around Kilmarnock in John Allan's native Scotland. There were many of "Pa's" relatives and friends to meet there, and he could romp across the countryside with Allan's young cousins, the Galt boys, who lived nearby on a great estate. It was the beautiful country of the Scottish poet Robert Burns, and of the romantic novelist Walter Scott. To Edgar, even as a young child, the lakes and parks, the lingering twilights and the reddish sunsets must have been inspiring sights. He stored them in his memory, along with the haunting shadows of the Scottish landscape; with stories of crumbling ancestral castles; and with the memory of "Pa" reciting Burns's lilting "Tam O'Shanter."

Next came stops at the cities: Glasgow, Edinburgh, and, finally, London. There were colorful scenes for Edgar to recall later—the street beggars and tramps; the peddlars hawking their wares; the armies of black-clad clerks.

But, at last, the excitement of touring had to end. With the Allans settled in adequate if not spacious London quarters, it was time to think again about Edgar's education. Seven years old, he was sent back to Irvine, Scotland, to school, despite his strong objections at having to leave the family. In his disappointment he even threatened to run away and return to America. The cause of his unhappiness, he declared, was "Pa," who would not agree to let him stay with "Mama" as she pleaded that he be allowed to do.

Edgar's school days in Scotland did not last long. Lonely and unhappy with the rigid discipline of his elementary school, he finally persuaded John Allan to send for him.

Allan next enrolled his strong-willed foster child in a school conducted by two sisters in the Chelsea section of London. Edgar was a boarding student, but he was able to visit with the Allans frequently at first. Then in August 1817, Frances Allan became ill and had to leave London for her health, recovering gradually at a fashionable resort. John Allan, now living alone, moved to smaller quarters. He asked Edgar to send his letters to "Mama," who was weak and no longer able to visit the boy at school.

Meanwhile, Allan's business was floundering. Instead of the great expansion of trade that most merchants had expected, the end of the Napoleonic wars had ushered in a period of depression and hard times. Commerce between the United States and Great Britain was slow to develop, partly because the United States enacted a protective tariff to keep out foreign goods. The firm of Ellis and Allan had invested heavily just to establish its

London operation. With unemployment stalking England it was impossible even to break even on the original outlay of capital.

Still, when Edgar reached the age of nine and had to move to a more advanced school, Allan placed him in the Manor House School at Stoke Newington, a fashionable suburb of London. The school, operated by the Reverend John Bransby, had an excellent academic reputation; it was also very expensive.

John Allan, obviously pleased with Edgar's exceptional success as a scholar, provided the boy—known in England as "Edgar Allan"—with ample spending money and such "extras" as a single bed apart from the general dormitory. The businesslike Allan had good reason to believe that his investment in Edgar's education was a sound one. Reading, study, and games of the mind were always matters of great pleasure to the quick-witted orphan boy. And up to this time his classmates had always liked him, even though he was usually acknowledged to be the best student.

Stoke Newington was an ancient village located on an old Roman road. Writing about it many years later Poe could still remember it well:

> I feel the refreshing chilliness of its deeply-shadowed avenues, inhale the fragrance of its thousand shrubberies, and thrill anew with indefinable delight, at the deep, hollow note of the churchbell, breaking each hour, with sud-

den and sullen roar, upon the stillness of the
dusky atmosphere in which the fretted Gothic
steeple lay imbedded and asleep.

The historic village was steeped in the romantic
atmosphere which even at the age of nine must
have pleased Poe. The Manor House School, like
most fine English academies of the day, provided
a rigorous, disciplined curriculum; it was here that
Poe first was held by his teachers to the standard
of precise, uncompromising excellence in the use
of language which was to be his passion. Sports
and games were an important part of life at the
school, too, especially cricket and the English version of football. In a word, Manor House should
have been a delight for young Edgar Allan Poe.

In fact, however, he detested it. Some of the
boys teased him about his American accent. Others were enraged to find him far ahead of them in
history and literature, because of unassigned reading he had done. Moreover, unlike most schoolboys, then as now, for whom learning a foreign
language is a dreary chore, Poe rapidly became
fluent in both written and spoken French; he
cared deeply about the beauty of the language.
There was also the matter of his separate bed,
away from most of his classmates in the dormitory;
this became a point of irritation even though it was
a customary "extra" among many such options
offered in British schools.

Probably for the first time in his life Poe did not emerge as a leader among his peers, except in academic matters. There was little that he could do to reverse the situation. He always had excelled as a swimmer, but the Reverend Bransby strictly prohibited his pupils from swimming in the nearby river. And the American Poe was unable to compete with skilled English schoolboys in their native field sports—although the cost of new shoes billed to John Allan suggests no shortage of effort on his part; he was active and athletic.

In defense, Poe retreated within himself. More than ever he took to reading alone when he was not scheduled for classes or games. Often he would peer through a high window of the school at a large, unusual, castlelike building across the street. It dated back perhaps to the Age of Elizabeth, more than two centuries earlier. He would gaze with fascination at the haphazardly placed dormers, the rambling wings and rooms branching out octopus-like from the main building, and at the scraggly ill-kept grounds where once there had been gracious formal gardens. He pondered the scene. What mysteries lay behind the ominous stone walls that surrounded the property? What tales of terror lurked in the meandering passageways? Young Poe, lonely and unpopular, began to create a fantasy world of moods, characters, and places in his lively imagination.

Sometimes his dreams would be interrupted by

the pealing chime of the big school clock calling him to class, or perhaps to the quaint chapel where stern John Bransby, majestically clothed in his black ministerial robes, would deliver a fiery sermon on good and evil.

Edgar's school days in England, so vital in shaping his personality, ended abruptly. John Allan's business fortunes were now plummeting. There had been a major theft of company funds in London, and even the American branch of Ellis and Allan was in the financial doldrums. Only by a stroke of good fortune was Allan able to conclude a final profitable deal in England and raise the money to book shipboard passage for himself and his family back to America. In May 1820, he withdrew Edgar from Manor House, and in the middle of June the Allans, with Miss Valentine and Edgar, sailed for New York from Liverpool aboard the *Martha.*

Edgar, now eleven years old, had learned much in England. Like most English schoolboys he knew how to use his fists to defend himself; he enjoyed playing jokes and pranks; and partly because of his travels, he had a poise and charm far beyond that of the American schoolmates he would soon encounter.

Intelligent and likeable, he was in many ways a healthy, outgoing boy. But there was another side to his nature, too. He was already a person of stubborn pride and sensitivity, a melancholy youngster frequently given over to morbid thoughts. He was quick to take offense at real or imaginary slights.

Even before his return to Richmond in August 1820, Edgar was searching for ways to express his ideas about life and death and beauty. He enjoyed sketching and painting, but was especially pleased to discover a growing delight in putting words on paper.

To his teachers in England it appeared that young "Edgar Allan," with his quick wit and winning manner, almost certainly was destined for a happy future.

# 2

## *the making of a virginia gentleman* (1820–1827)

Just as Edgar stored in his memory the street scenes of crowded London and the misty lanes of Stoke Newington, he absorbed the lessons of the ocean voyage home. Always adventurous, he immersed himself in sea lore, listening with rapt attention to the fantastic stories of the sailors and picturing in his mind the exotic people and places they described. After more than a month at sea the twelve-year-old Poe had the details for exciting stories of his own that he would first tell to wide-eyed schoolmates in Richmond and years later would write out for publication.

In the early 1820s Richmond had a population of about twelve thousand persons. After the frenetic bustle of London it must have seemed quietly provincial to the perceptive Edgar. Still, it was a good place to be a young boy. Edgar and his chums could romp in the woods, swim in the nearby creeks and streams, organize fish frys by the James River, go to masquerades, play cards; the variety of pleasant diversions was endless.

The Tidewater area of Virginia was, above all, a place of aristocracy and tradition. Inherited wealth and family lineage were prized. And the ideal of every growing boy of rank was to become a "Virginia gentleman." The term implied a code of honor—in payment of one's debts, with regard to women, and in common admiration for fine horsemanship and military bearing. Richmond's social life was gracious, and impeccable manners were a mark of cultivation expected of any family of rank. Each family, too, was aware of the precise rung on which it stood in Richmond's social ladder.

John Allan, vain and ambitious, knew his social standing and resented it. Thus, although the affairs of Ellis and Allan continued to suffer, Allan insisted on enrolling his foster son in the fashionable English and Classical School of Joseph W. Clarke. The cost of Edgar's tuition and books amounted to only sixty dollars a year, but in those days the dollar bought many times what it does today. The sum unquestionably represented a sacrifice for Allan, and during the year 1822 he had to pay the bill in installments. Clearly then, it was still important to him at that date to provide Edgar with an education suitable for the life of a gentleman.

Headmaster Joseph Clarke knew what parents expected him to serve up to his young charges.

The curriculum consisted of Latin, French, and mathematics, with a smattering of classic English literature. As usual, Poe was far beyond his classmates. Sometime between the ages of twelve and fourteen he began to write poetry in earnest—secretly, of course, for fear of being teased by his male friends. The result was mostly verses of lyric love, closely aping the style of Byron, and reflecting his growing interest in women as he entered adolescence.

Poetry was only one part of Edgar's life as a teenager. He enjoyed hunting and fishing. Once he enticed Tom Ellis, the ten-year-old son of his foster father's business partner, to shoot fowl with him on the private estate of Judge Bushrod Washington. Caught, Tom escaped punishment at home, but for once Mama and Aunt Nancy were unable to shield Edgar from John Allan's wrath; the boy received a sound whipping. Nevertheless Tom continued to idolize Edgar—even after Poe threw him into deep water to teach him how to swim and then had to rescue him from drowning.

Edgar became something of a local hero for an athletic feat he performed at the age of fifteen. One hot June day he swam six miles up the James River to Warwick against one of the strongest tides ever known in the river. A crowd of his classmates and many townspeople lined the riverbank to cheer him on. As late as 1835, Poe still was writing about the deed.

According to contemporary accounts Edgar Allan Poe was an accomplished, accepted young person—bright, graceful, attractive, polished. In the ancestor-conscious South, however, he was never allowed to forget his origins. Sometimes he had to use his fists against schoolmates to defend the honor of his dead mother, considered disreputable because she had been an actress. Perhaps he was sensitive, too, about bringing home to the unpretentious cottage of John Allan his circle of friends from the best families. It was not that a refined Cabell, Thomas, Preston, or Selden would have snubbed him directly; rather that in the precisely defined social structure of the city he was destined always to remain the outsider—"Edgar Poe," rather than "Edgar Allan," as he had been welcomed in England.

Nevertheless, to Tom Ellis and many of the younger boys, the handsome, well proportioned Poe, with his charming and somewhat mysterious ways, stood out as an object of veneration. One of the boys who idolized him was Rob Stanard. And it was on an after-school visit to Rob's home that Edgar met Jane Stith Stanard, Rob's mother. The meeting marked a turning point in the budding poet's life.

Almost at once Poe became devoted to the beautiful, elegantly mannered Mrs. Stanard. He was captivated by her warmth and charm, and deeply moved by the sympathy and intelligent concern she showed for his poetry. In recognition of the classical beauty that he saw in her Edgar asked to call her "Helen" rather than Jane—for the Greek Helen of Troy. She agreed.

Perhaps the fifteen-year-old Poe found in Mrs. Stanard—although she was scarcely into her thirties—the motherly compassion that he had lost when his own mother died. Unquestionably, too, he discovered in her the image of womanhood that filled his idealistic longing for feminine beauty and purity. Poe was sensitive and romantic. Mrs. Stanard was a heroine who combined in real life all of his fondest dreams.

From what is known, "Helen" responded to young Edgar with just the proper blend of distance and wise encouragement for his work.

One result of the relationship would be Poe's immortal poem, "To Helen," which he polished for the rest of his life. In it are some of his most famous lines, beginning "Helen, thy beauty is to me," and including his oft-quoted praise for the woman who summed up for him the essence of classic civilization: "The glory that was Greece/ And the grandeur that was Rome."

Day after day Edgar visited the stately home of Jane Stanard. He and "Helen" shared a zest for life's beauty, tinged with the melancholy sadness of their personalities. Both were delicately balanced, sensitive, vulnerable. Both were seekers after perfection in an imperfect world. For a critical moment—perhaps a year—when Edgar's own development as an artist hung in the balance, he was deliriously happy, intoxicated by the inspiration of the statuesque Helen.

On April 28, 1824, with jarring suddenness, Jane Stith Stanard died of a brain tumor.

Edgar was crushed. For weeks afterward he and Rob Stanard, singly and in each other's company, visited the grave, sometimes at night. The fifteen-year-old Poe could not—would not—believe that death had taken from him his ideal love. Again, as with his mother, death had robbed him of happiness and affection. Death, the macabre horror of the graveyard, the terror of the cold hand on one's forehead in total darkness, burial—these became underlying elements of Poe's craft. Finally they would become the essence of his genius.

Edgar had found in Helen an understanding that eluded him in his own home. Frances Allan had neither the intelligence nor the sensitivity to appreciate her foster son's poetry. John Allan, although proud enough of the boy's writing to show a notebook of it to some of his business friends, thought of scribbling poetry as largely an impractical waste of time, and maybe even a little "unmanly." The attitude was symptomatic of a larger problem. As Edgar advanced into adolescence and then early manhood, his relationship with his alternately harsh and gentle Scottish guardian changed. Their contacts became markedly more strained. The tension in the household mounted with each passing month.

In 1824 when Lafayette visited Richmond, a volunteer military unit served as his honorary escort. It was made up of young men from the town's most respected families. Poe, chosen as lieutenant, was second in command. As the grandson of "General Poe," Lafayette's comrade, he may have met the French hero and been led to recall with pride his own ancestry.

With growing independence, too, he began to widen his acquaintanceship in Richmond. Inevitably he would have learned, as his foster mother already had, that John Allan was well known among the loose women of the town. It was also rumored that the progressive illness from which Allan was suffering was a venereal disease.

To the idealistic Poe, grateful to Frances Allan for rescuing him when he was a helpless orphan, the revelation of the family head's infidelities must have been a severe shock. Within the Allan household there was now hostility—ugly charges and countercharges. "Aunt Nancy" Valentine, aware that her sister continued in poor health and that she might some day have to depend on John Allan for financial support, sided with Allan. Edgar loyally sided with his "mother," which Allan deeply resented, labeling it "ingratitude."

It was about this time, too, that Edgar quickened the sporadic correspondence he had been conducting with his older brother, Henry. Since returning from England Edgar had often seen his sister, Rosalie, who still lived in apparent happiness with the Mackenzies in Richmond. Quite unexplainably Rosalie's mental growth stopped when she was fourteen, and for the rest of her life she remained alert but abnormally "slow." Henry Poe, like Edgar, wrote both prose and verse, although he was forced to make his way in the world working at odd jobs and as a sailor. He was pleased to visit occasionally with the more fortunate Edgar at the comfortable Allan home.

John Allan vindictively took advantage of Edgar's renewed friendship with his brother. He wrote to Henry, describing the sixteen-year-old Edgar as "miserable, sulky & ill-tempered." "The boy," he said, "possesses not a spark of affection for us, not a particle of gratitude for all my care and kindliness toward him. I have given [sic] a much superior Education than ever I received myself. . . ."*

Perhaps John Allan hoped to convince Henry that Edgar really was ungrateful. Then the older brother might be able to silence Edgar's complaints about his foster father's extramarital affairs. If this was the Scotsman's purpose it did

---

*Allan also tried to hint that Rosalie was really the illegitimate daughter of Elizabeth Poe and John Howard Payne, an actor. This may well have been a poorly kept family secret.

not work. Edgar had sympathy for his "Mama," contempt for his "Pa"; and he would not hide his feelings out of fear or because of petty gossip.

In the spring of 1825, the Allans' domestic wrangling suddenly—if temporarily—stopped. John Allan's wealthy uncle, William Galt, died, leaving him the bulk of an estate worth more than three quarters of a million dollars. Overnight, Allan's financial worries were over. He was one of Virginia's wealthiest men.

The Allans moved to a mansion at the corner of Fifth and Main Streets, long to be identified as "Allan House." They furnished the house magnificently and began entertaining with a lavishness extraordinary even by Southern standards. Edgar shared in the family's good fortune. He dressed in the most stylish fashions, had Negro slaves to cater to his every wish, and ordered imported books and periodicals for his growing library. To the beautiful young girls of Richmond he stood out as a particularly "eligible" bachelor.

Edgar usually showed little interest in the girls who set their sights on him. But one girl succeeded in capturing his attention. She was Sarah Elmira Royster, or as he called her, "Myra." Sixteen, like Edgar, she had large, dark eyes and silky black hair parted in the middle. There was about her an air of romantic sadness, a melancholy which characterized Poe's taste in women.

Edgar would take Myra to a shaded garden,

walled in by honeysuckle and roses, to speak with her of love and to tell her of his dreams of literary fame. Sometimes he would play the flute for her or sketch her face in pencil. Later, in his story "The Landscape Garden," he was to recreate the setting with loving memory, calling it "the secret garden."

In 1826, when the two were seventeen, they became secretly engaged. It was, Poe later recalled, a sweet, "innocent" love. A young man of privilege, handsome, strikingly intelligent, groomed for the life of the Virginia aristocracy, Poe had the world before him—including the love of a desirable girl.

Soon, however, he was to begin a new and very different period in his life. On February 12, 1826, with his foster mother at his side in a carriage, Edgar Allan Poe left Richmond to enroll in Charlottesville at the promising new University of Virginia, founded only one year before by Thomas Jefferson himself.

Even today few college campuses in the United States can equal the stately beauty of the University of Virginia. When Poe arrived the imposing classical rotunda, conceived by Jefferson, was not yet complete. But the other features which make the college physically distinctive were ready: the vast lawns, the symmetrical courtyards rimmed by spacious faculty residences, and the orderly "ranges" of student rooms, each with its fireplace and clean, white, plastered walls. The shrubs and plantings, laid out under Jefferson's personal supervision, enhanced the atmosphere of quiet dignity.

Student life at the university was anything but dignified. Fighting, drinking, gambling, and dueling were the order of the day. And the superb faculty of erudite European scholars imported by Jefferson to staff his fledgling institution were at a loss to restore order among the Virginia "gentlemen" in attendance. Many of the first students had enrolled only at their parents' demand and were more intent on cultivating their own particular bad habits than on obtaining higher learning. Some even brought their own horses, dogs, and private servants. Only a serious few made use of the library.

Poe, on the other hand, worked hard. His classes were scheduled from seven to nine in the morning, leaving him a full day for his scholarly pursuits. He worked through the summer and then took examinations in the fall term. The results must have pleased him—a second place in Latin and first place in French. He even won the grudging praise of his exacting European professors.

From the start, however, Poe was in deep financial trouble at the university. John Allan had bestowed on him a handshake and his best wishes when he set out from Richmond, but only $110 in cash. Concessionaires demanded more than $150 for supplying laundry, meals, and servants. Tuition for his lectures in French and Latin was $60, making it impossible for him to register for mathematics, too, the only course John Allan thought worthwhile.

Immediately Edgar wrote to Allan, detailing specifically the costs he was encountering. Allan responded, grudgingly forwarding a check—but for only $40, enough to pay the bare minimum deposits on services, but leaving Poe with only one dollar pocket money for the year. None of his "son's" arguments succeeded in moving the wealthy Scotsman from his position of tightfistedness—a policy intended perhaps to drive Poe away, or—as always before—to break his pride and make him subservient. Allan apparently was torn between his devotion to the youngster and his desire not to be committed.

With no other choice, Poe began to borrow from the local merchants of Charlottesville, drawing upon his reputation as a "rich man's son." Still without funds and deeply in debt he next tried his luck at cards. He lost. In an effort to recoup his losses he risked still greater amounts. By the middle of the fall term he owed over $2,500.

Meanwhile, Poe had heard nothing from Elmira Royster. As he later discovered, his letters to her were intercepted by her parents. She in turn thought that he had lost interest in their romance.

The sweet but weak-willed Elmira gave in to her parents' arguments that she marry A. Barrett Shelton, a wealthy young man from one of Richmond's most socially acceptable families. But neither she nor Poe's family wanted to break the unpleasant news to him. Yet, sensitive, he had a nagging suspicion that his romance with Elmira was finished.

Embittered that Elmira had apparently forgotten him and eager to emulate the wealthy planters' sons at the university, Poe now took to occasional drinking. It was not that he particularly liked the taste of alcohol; he did not. Rather he enjoyed its effect—the forgetfulness it brought him. Even small amounts of alcohol, however, made him excruciatingly ill. Or as was then said, "Less than a little was with him too much." Sometimes he would not even remember later what he had done while under the influence of drink.

By the middle of the fall term creditors began pressing Edgar Poe's wealthy "father" for payment of the boy's debts, including his losses at cards. John Allan refused to pay a cent of the money owed from gambling, although Edgar protested that those were "debts of honor" to his friends; if they were left unpaid he would lose all respectability at the university. Moreover, Poe bitterly observed, gambling would have been unnecessary if Allan had only given him enough money in the first place to meet his expenses.

Just before the Christmas holidays Edgar prepared to leave Charlottesville. He packed all of his books and manuscripts, as well as his clothing. The night before he was to return to Richmond with a group of fellow students he burned the last furniture in his room as firewood. He was that certain that John Allan would never allow him to return to the university. With forebodings of harder days to come he said farewell to Room Number 13, West Range (today maintained as a shrine to him) and to the University of Virginia.

In Richmond, over the holidays, his worst fears were confirmed. Elmira was gone from the city—married to Shelton. Poe was shattered. His love for her had been real, and her loss was a major crisis in his life. Not only was his pride damaged but also he was diverted from his plan to settle early into family life. Instead of the lifetime commitment that marriage then was supposed to represent, he was faced with uncertainty. In time, the uncertainty would become rootlessness.

Next, he received another blow. The estimated bills for the year 1827 at the university were released, totaling $233, not including personal expenses. Edgar had only $150. The question of Edgar's occupational choice now reached a head. He could not return to the university without help. John Allan spoke of his entering law school, but Edgar refused even to consider it; he had his mind set on a literary career. There was much wrangling. Many a father-son relationship has been wrecked on the shoals of just such a conflict in career aspirations.

On March 18, 1827, Poe and his foster father had an explosive argument. Allan again accused Edgar of ingratitude. He brought up the matter of the gambling debts and Poe's drinking, saying that they had done damage to the family's name. Edgar replied with sarcasm that Allan's extramarital affairs had done far more damage than a few drinks of "peach and honey" in Charlottesville.

The argument grew more heated. Then, raising his cane threateningly, Allan shouted at his ward to leave the house. Edgar was stunned. But on an impulse he turned and abruptly left. It was to be the decisive moment in Poe's life.

Once outside the door of Allan House, Edgar had no place to go. The Roysters had treated him with contempt when, after first returning to Richmond, he called to inquire about his beloved "Myra." For a person of his pride it was out of the question to seek refuge with any of Allan's relatives. Desolate, he went to the Court House Tavern. But unable to pay for a room or buy a meal he simply made arrangements to pick up his mail there under the alias "Henri le Rennét." This was intended partly to elude his creditors in an age when debtors were unceremoniously thrown into prison. It was also for his own self-regard, to demonstrate a firm resolution to carve out a life of his own—"le Rennét" being his humorous twist on the French for "the reborn."

That very evening Poe drafted a letter to John Allan, addressing his once revered "Pa" as "Sir." "My determination," he said, "is at length taken— to leave your house and indeavor [sic] to find some place in the wide world, where I will be treated— not as *you* have treated me." He asked for his trunk with all of his clothing and books, and enough money to live for a month in some Northern city where he might start a new life.

Allan replied, restating his own position that Poe had been ungrateful, but sending neither money nor the trunk. By now Poe had missed several meals; he pleaded for Allan's assistance in paying for transportation out of Richmond. This time the bitter foster father did not even answer his ward's letter, but with petty anger added an "s" to the boy's signature, Poe, in reference to Edgar's "pose." Then after scrawling "Pretty Letter" at the top of the message, he filed it with his business correspondence.

Somehow—probably through the loving Mrs. Allan—Poe found enough money to leave Richmond. He made his way to Boston, the city of his birth, some accounts say by working on a coal barge.

By mid-April, alone, virtually penniless, but with high hopes and persistence, Edgar was tramping purposefully across Boston Common, eager to find a publisher for a slim volume of his work entitled *Tamerlane and Other Poems.*

The title poem told the story of a dying conqueror who, because of high ambition, had left behind both his childhood sweetheart and his home, finally losing both. Like his own portrait of Tamerlane, Poe had lost Elmira as well as his home. But at eighteen, adventurous and incurably romantic, he was still convinced that the world was his to conquer.

# 3

## *poet in khaki*
## (1827–1831)

*Tamerlane and Other Poems* appeared in May
1827. It was a slim volume of only some forty
pages, measuring $6^3/_8$ by $4^1/_8$ inches, and bound in
light-brown covers. Poe could afford to have only
forty or fifty copies run off the press of Calvin F. S.
Thomas, a nineteen-year-old printer newly open
for business. Of these, he sent a few copies out for
review and was forced to keep the rest; nobody
would buy them. Today a copy of the book's first
edition would bring thousands of dollars at auc-
tion.

Probably to conceal himself from his creditors,
Poe published this first book anonymously. The
title page bore only the designation "By a Bostoni-
an." Still the young poet must have experienced
some satisfaction at seeing his words in print.*

The inner glow was no substitute, however, for

*Even major American publishing houses at that time tried to
minimize their risks by requiring authors to underwrite the basic costs

food and shelter. Reduced to desperate straits after seven weeks in Boston, Poe enlisted for a five-year term in the United States Army. He used the alias "Edgar A. Perry." Although still only eighteen, he claimed to be twenty-two years old. War Department records specify that at the time of his enlistment he was five feet, eight inches tall, had gray eyes, brown hair, and a fair complexion. For an occupation he listed himself as "clerk."

Poe was assigned to Battery H of the First Artillery Regiment, then stationed in Boston Harbor. If nothing else he was assured of regular meals, clothes on his back, and a roof over his head. The sensitive lad, reared to be a Southern gentleman, dutifully responded to the jarring call of reveille at 5:30 in the morning. He learned to drill, to clean and fire the big guns protecting Boston Harbor, and, working alongside men who had labored in fields and on the docks, to do the hundreds of coarse, dirty jobs that necessarily must be done in the army.

His education and obvious intelligence made him stand out from his comrades, and soon won

---

of publication. Such a guarantee was common in dealing with authors unknown to the public—particularly poets, since poetry was a notoriously slow-selling category of work. Poe ingeniously managed to raise the necessary cash payment. Like many of the "hippies" of the late 1960s, he often lived on the edge of "genteel poverty," borrowing from well-to-do friends or relatives with no intention of ever repaying the money. When, as in this period in his life, he could no longer look to home for help, his situation grew really serious.

him certain privileges. Trusted, he became company clerk, handling the Battery's books and records. He mastered that job quickly and learned to finish his day's work in a few hours. Then he used his leisure time to dream and to write.

In November 1827, Poe's unit was transferred by sea to Fort Moultrie, in the harbor of Charleston, South Carolina. There he spent his happiest days in the army. The warm Southern climate pleased him. He found the aristocratic old city of Charleston both enchanting and hospitable. It was opened to him, despite his lowly rank, by two new acquaintances he made in the area: Colonel William Drayton, a politician, and Dr. Edmund Ravenel, a naturalist living on nearby Sullivan's Island.

Drayton, charmed by Private Poe's graceful manners and broad knowledge, introduced him to the leaders of Charleston society. The young poet found himself a welcome visitor to fine old mansions around the city. He enjoyed noting how the trees marking their approaches were draped romantically with Spanish moss. It was a slow, languid atmosphere, one in which Poe moved with accustomed ease.

Dr. Ravenel, meanwhile, was opening for him the mysteries of science along the broad, white stretch of oceanfront on Sullivan's Island. It was there that Poe learned the details of plant and animal classification. The island, vividly photographed in Poe's memory, many years later would provide the setting for "The Gold Bug," one of his most famous stories. Indeed, the extraordinary beetle of the story was modeled after an insect which Dr. Ravenel once encountered while exploring a thicket near the beach in Poe's company.

Under the influence of Ravenel, Poe read science; Drayton led him to modern literature. His regard for Lord Byron's muscular romanticism gave way to admiration for the subtleties of Wordsworth and Coleridge. He became intrigued with the Koran and Muslim literature. Out of this period of army service came his "Sonnet—To Science" and the mystical, imaginative poem "Al Aaraaf."

"Private Perry" was a successful soldier. In May 1828 he was promoted to "artificer," a rank which carried few new duties but meant higher pay and still more leisure time. His officers, impressed with his attention to duty and his outstanding ability, moved him quickly through the noncommissioned ranks. On January 1, 1829, not yet twenty, he was appointed sergeant-major, the highest grade below officer rank. By then the regiment had moved to Fortress Monroe, near Norfolk, Virginia.

Despite his progress Poe appears to have grown impatient with army life. He began expressing a desire to spend more time on his writing before he "passed his prime." Somehow he managed to start a correspondence once again with John Allan. This time he asked only that his foster father request his early release from the service, a matter which legally could be arranged through a parent or guardian. Allan, however, may have been reluctant to permit the sharp-tongued Edgar to intrude in his life again; he replied that a military career was precisely what the lad needed.

A rapid deterioration of Frances Allan's health changed the marble-hearted businessman's mind. "Ma" pleaded with her husband to do what he could for Edgar, at least to help him leave the service. To please John Allan, Poe proposed an alternative: he would enroll at West Point and become an officer. This, he thought, would endear him again to "Pa." The life of an army officer was then a leisurely, gentleman's existence, provided of course that the officer had an independent outside income. Poe gambled that, with Allan's support, he could win a commission and then later return to writing. After all, even a small inheritance from the wealthy merchant would make possible the free time he needed for his writing career.

Always cautious, John Allan hesitated. At first he did not answer Edgar's letters about West Point. But events forced him to act. His wife's situation suddenly became critical. Allan wrote to his foster son asking him to come at once. By now Sergeant "Perry's" officers had learned the truth about his background, and had encouraged him in his plan to attend West Point. They arranged for an emergency, ten-day furlough for him to be with his foster mother in her illness.

Knowing that she was close to death, Frances Allan declared as her last wish that she not be buried before her "dear boy," Edgar, had been allowed to look upon her face once more. Frantically Poe raced to Richmond by stagecoach. He rushed up the front stairs of Allan House and threw open the door.

He was too late.

On February 28, 1829, "Ma" had died. Despite her wishes she was buried before Edgar could see her. The day after his arrival he visited the cemetery—the very cemetery where Mrs. Stanard was buried—and wept by the grave of his "mother."

Here was the third woman to whom he had looked for affection only to have her taken from him by death: first his mother, then Mrs. Stanard, and now the woman who had reared him and protected him—Frances Allan. Poe's tender, sensitive nature had been dealt still another cruel blow.

For some time after his wife's death John Allan tried to live up to her plea that he not desert Edgar. The grieving merchant provided his ward with a suit of black mourning clothes. Then he sympathetically discussed with him the advantages of entering West Point—one of which, no doubt, was that the United States government would assume the expense of the boy's upbringing. Still, at least for the moment, Edgar and his "Pa" were reconciled. Once again Edgar was able to sign with the word "affectionately" his letters to the man who in crucial ways still controlled his destiny.

Poe's next task was to find a substitute to take his place in the army. Ordinarily this might have cost him only a twelve-dollar bounty fee, usually paid to the first recruit who appeared to sign the enlistment book. But all of Fortress Monroe's senior officers were away when Poe returned to the base, and he was in a hurry. To avoid a delay of several days he was obliged to pay a full bounty to a long-term veteran, Sergeant Samuel "Bully" Graves, for reenlisting. The fee was seventy-five dollars, of which he gave Graves twenty-five dollars in cash and the rest in the form of a promissory note. Twelve dollars, he recalled, ruefully, was the figure he had quoted to John Allan as the cost of a substitute. But thinking that under the circumstances he had little choice, Poe proceeded with the formalities of his discharge from service.

"Sergeant Perry" received an honorable discharge from the United States Army on April 15, 1829. His lieutenant wrote him a warm letter of recommendation, including the statement that, "His habits are good and entirely free from drinking."

Somewhat less glowing was John Allan's letter to Secretary of War John Eaton recommending his foster son for admission to West Point. In it he noted that Poe had left him after incurring gambling debts at the University of Virginia. "Frankly, sir, do I declare," said Allan, "that he is no relation to me whatever." Although there were many others in whom he had taken an interest, continued Allan (probably thinking of his illegitimate children), he was still willing to recommend that Poe be given consideration for West Point. "Pardon my frankness," he concluded to the Secretary of War, "but I address a soldier." Perhaps because of his wealthy guardian's lukewarm recommendation, Poe's application to West Point was dutifully filed away at theWar Department and for many months received no attention.

Poe had anticipated no difficulty in winning appointment to the military academy. While waiting for formal notification of his acceptance, he went to live in Baltimore. There he intended to arrange for publication of a second volume of his poems, including "Al Aaraaf." His closest relatives, moreover, were in Baltimore, and since John Allan supplied him with only meager sums of money at irregular intervals he often found it convenient to stay with them.

Waiting to greet Edgar were his grandmother Mrs. David Poe (wife of the "General"), his aunt

Mrs. Maria Clemm, and Mrs. Clemm's seven-year-old daughter, Virginia. By this time Poe's grandmother was aged and helpless. The entire household was nevertheless dependent on the twenty-dollar-a-month pension check the "General's" widow received from the government. The thirty-nine-year-old Mrs. Clemm devoted herself almost exclusively to the care of the elderly woman. To make the situation even more precarious Edgar's brother, William Henry Leonard Poe, also lived with the family much of the time. He had returned from a career at sea too frail to work and hopelessly addicted to alcohol. Despite the family's depressing condition Edgar, now twenty-one, found himself caught up in the kindness and affection of those he considered closest to him by lasting ties of blood.To one tossed about for so long among strangers it was a heartwarming feeling.

Through the help of a prominent lawyer he had met at the University of Virginia, Edgar made contact with a Philadelphia publisher, Carey, Lea & Carey. The firm was willing to print his second volume of poems. But because poetry usually sold so slowly, they asked a guarantee of one hundred dollars from Poe to protect themselves against loss. Knowing nowhere else to turn for help, Poe wrote to John Allan for the money. He couched his request in humble, apologetic terms and pointed out that the project not only would put his name in the public eye but might also turn a profit. Allan rudely spurned his foster son's plea, and even accused him of "bad conduct."

Poe withdrew his manuscript from Carey, Lea & Carey. But he doggedly persisted, next sending some of the poems to John Neal, editor of the *Yankee and Boston Literary Gazette.* Neal was pleased with the poems and arranged to have them published by Hatch and Dunning, a Baltimore firm. In December 1829, Poe's second volume of poems appeared under the title *Al Aaraaf, Tamerlane, and Minor Poems.* The older works, including "Tamerlane," had been almost completely reworked and polished, a practice Poe always followed with his poetry. The poems now were more melancholy, as well as more personal, reflecting some of Edgar's unfortunate loves for women now gone from his life or dead. Often, too, their meaning was obscure. This was intentional. Poe was concerned with creating moods, not teaching lessons. Even this early in his career he declared that the purpose of poetry was to give pleasure and to transmit visions, never to be objective.

The critical response to Poe's new book encouraged him greatly. One review, although negative, compared him to Shelley; another spoke of his "genius." Around Baltimore he was asked to give readings of his works and sometimes even to sign autographs.

Still there was no money coming in, and no

word from West Point—upon which (he thought at the time) "Pa's" favor depended. One fearfully hot day in July, Edgar started out on foot from Baltimore to Washington. Arriving at the office of the Secretary of War, Edgar gained admission and spoke personally to the cabinet official. Ten potential West Point cadets, he learned, were ahead of him, but dropouts from the academy were numerous in the summertime because of the rigorous outdoor activities. With that tiny grain of inconclusive information for his trouble, Edgar Allan Poe turned on his heel and began to walk back to Baltimore.

In January 1830, John Allan agreed to let Edgar visit with him in Richmond. Upon the young poet's arrival Allan fitted him with new clothing and gave him spending money. Nevertheless the two continued to quarrel. This time there was a new issue: Poe had persuaded Allan's sister-in-law, "Aunt Nancy" Valentine, to refuse the Scotsman's offer of marriage. Allan was exasperated at his ward's continued interference. He was tired, too, of what he considered Poe's cavalier attitude toward money.

But Allan had other problems than his proud ward with literary pretensions. His idle bachelor hours had brought him in contact with Mrs. Elizabeth Wills, who in July 1830, would present him with a set of twins. Meanwhile, he had courted and won the hand of Miss Louisa Gabriella Patterson, a strong-willed spinster of thirty from an aristocratic New York family. In view of these new connections, Allan was eager to have done with the critical Edgar Poe, so ready to sit as judge of his foster father's morality.

Allan was delighted therefore when government officials informed him in the late spring of 1830 of the youth's acceptance to West Point. After taking Edgar to the steamboat for the trip north, he may have breathed a sigh of relief. The sensitive Poe probably understood his foster father's feelings, since he later wrote, "When I parted from you—at the steam-boat, I knew that I should never see you again."

Allan's parting gift to the boy he once was proud to claim in place of a natural heir was twenty dollars in spending money and four blankets from the stock of Ellis and Allan.

By the end of June, Poe had arrived at West Point, poised in castlelike majesty on enormous palisades commanding the Hudson River. The view, as Poe would later recall, was splendid, if one had time to spare from one's studies and the onerous duties of cadet life to enjoy it. Nevertheless, the young Virginia poet, already an experienced soldier and scholar, easily passed his entrance examinations. On July 1, 1830, he swore to uphold and protect the Constitution of the United States of America and formally became a cadet at the United States Military Academy.

In October 1830, Allan married the strong-willed Miss Patterson in New York City. Poe hoped that his foster father would make the short trip up the Hudson to West Point following the wedding. But Allan did not even answer his ward's invitation. Apparently he considered the association at an end.

Meanwhile Poe was in his usual financial quagmire. Out of a monthly allowance of twenty-eight dollars, cadets were expected to pay for their own books, clothing, engineering instruments, and all incidentals, including even soap and candles. Customarily, parents placed a certain sum of money on deposit to cover such items. But not John Allan, who refused even to answer his young charge's pleas for help.

Just as at the University of Virginia, Poe soon found himself in debt to his classmates. One by one he sold off the blankets his guardian had given him until his room, already bare of possessions, took on the aspect of a cell.

Poe had made one other miscalculation in coming to West Point. He had assumed that because of his military experience and superior intellectual attainments he would be able to breeze through the Academy's curriculum in "perhaps six months." He was correct in expecting an advantage. At the age of twenty-two he was older and certainly more experienced than even the senior cadets. Drill and other soldierly routines were child's play for him. And with only minimal study he excelled in his academic work, particularly French and mathematics. Sometimes he would not study until he entered the classroom and then just glance at the day's assignment to master it.

But other aspects of life at "The Point" were harder to control. From the sound of reveille at dawn to taps at 9:30 there was an inescapable round of physical exercise, parades, roll calls, and formally scheduled classes. Rigid discipline prevailed, even at meals. And the hazing of Plebes— first-year cadets—provided a source of continuing pleasure for upperclassmen, especially when the victim was as resentful and aloof as Poe. To his irritation Edgar discovered that he had none of the time for solitude and reverie that he had enjoyed as an enlisted man. With every day that slipped past him with little or no opportunity for writing, his frustration increased.

According to the rules of the military academy, smoking, drinking, and card playing were forbidden. This in itself was a sufficient challenge for adventurous cadets to make their way to "Benny's" or one of the other off-limits establishments where they could find release from rigorous discipline and their Spartan living quarters.

Poe was nervous and irritable from the constant interruption of his thoughts. Slight of frame, easily fatigued, he could not meet the demands the West Point life placed on him. Once again, in a crisis situation, Poe began to drink.

Never was it more than an occasional bottle of brandy smuggled in from Benny's. But as usual in his case, even a little was too much. Brooding in his room, Number 28 South Barracks, Poe questioned whether his entrapment in the confusion and triviality of the academy made sense.

A letter from John Allan forced his decision to leave. Before arriving at West Point Poe had written to "Bully" Graves, the sergeant at Fortress Monroe who had charged seventy-five dollars to act as Poe's substitute. Edgar had promised to pay "Bully" the amount still due on his note as soon as he could get the money from his guardian. But, he continued foolishly, "Mr. A is not very often sober." Hopeful of collecting his money, Graves sent the letter to John Allan. Furious over Poe's outrageous conduct in discussing intimate family matters with a stranger, Allan wrote to him declaring that he was disinherited, could expect nothing at all as a legacy. Furthermore, added Allan, he never again wanted to hear from Edgar Poe.

The letter was a body blow to the already discouraged young poet. In a bitter reply to his former guardian Poe indignantly recalled all of his old grievances. And, with more than a little self-pity, he thanked God that because of ill health his agony would be relieved by an early death. For now he asked of Allan only a letter permitting him to resign from the Academy, thereby entitling him to mileage money home. Otherwise, Edgar announced, he would neglect his duties in order to be dismissed.

Before Allan could answer, Poe deliberately began to absent himself from roll calls and refused to obey orders. The last regular West Point court-martial of the year was to meet on January 28, 1831, to try the cases of cadets accused of various breeches of military discipline. On January 7, Poe's name was placed on the list of cadets to be prosecuted. Prior to the trial, Poe broke every regulation that he could to be sure to accumulate sufficiently serious charges to make his conviction certain.

Now at last he spent all of his time writing and polishing his work, nearing the completion of a third volume of poetry. Eventually included in it was the haunting "Israfel," drawn from the Koran's discussion of the archangel of the Lord, Israfel, who surpassed all other creatures in the beauty of his song. A deeply moving stanza lays bare Poe's longing and his unhappiness:

> If I could dwell
> Where Israfel
>     Hath dwelt, and he where I,

> He might not sing so wildly well
>   A mortal melody,
> While a bolder note than this might swell
>   From my lyre within the sky.

Colonel Thayer, the superintendent of the military academy, knew of Poe's writing and was sympathetic to his ambitions. Thayer allowed Edgar to take subscriptions from among his fellow cadets for the new book at the price of seventy-five cents per copy; nearly every member of the cadet corps subscribed. A publisher from New York, Elam Bliss, visited West Point at Poe's invitation and contracted with Poe for the volume, perhaps attracted by the prospect of an assured advance sale of several hundred copies.

The cadets probably were less enticed by the glories of poetry than by Poe's glamorous, mysterious personality. The colorful youth had embellished the already exotic truth about his past with the outrageous claim that he was descended on his mother's side from the Revolutionary War traitor, Benedict Arnold, and that he had traveled to Greece and Russia on his own. Nor did he openly discourage the fond hopes of the cadets that he would lampoon the academy's officers in print, as he so often had done in light-hearted barracks verse.

At the court-martial proceedings he pleaded guilty to the charges against him, "gross neglect of duty" and "disobedience of orders." He was dismissed from the United States military academy.

On February 19, 1831, former cadet Edgar A. Poe stood shivering on the wharf at West Point waiting for the steamboat to New York. He was wrapped in his cadet greatcoat, draped incongruously over the lightweight summer clothing he had worn when he first arrived at the Academy. Ill with a severe cold and a badly infected ear, trembling, he was a picture of abject misery.

Perhaps as he waited on the dock Poe's thoughts turned to John Allan whose stubbornness, parsimony, and need to dominate had played such an important part in bringing him to his present situation. Or perhaps he thought of the mutual bond of affection that had held the two complicated men together so long and always before prevented them from making a clean, complete break.

But Poe was a fiercely proud young man. While he looked back to the easy luxury of his life with the Allans in Richmond his fertile mind almost certainly was at work wrestling with the problems of the new life he was about to begin. His last letter to John Allan had been a ringing declaration of artistic and financial independence. Meanwhile Elam Bliss had promised to publish his book of poems, a promise which could not help but raise his spirits.

The steamboat came into view around the bend

of the Hudson and slowly drew to shore, the sound of its whistle reverberating against the jagged rocks that rose precipitously from the river. As he trudged up the gangplank and into the welcome warmth of the lower deck, Poe, confident in his ability, was sure that the future—no matter what it brought—would be of his own making, not someone else's.

# 4

## *the wandering scribe*
## (1831–1837)

In the decade of the 1830s, the United States experienced dramatic physical and social changes. Settlers moved westward at an ever quickening pace. They swarmed into the Ohio River valley and the new lands added by the Louisiana Purchase. Whole new towns grew up overnight. Building was taking place everywhere—new houses, new stores, new schools. Since the time of Poe's birth in 1809, one new invention had followed another—first the railroad, then the steamboat, then the high-speed printing press. People's lives were speeded up.

The America of Poe's childhood, the America guided by that remarkable succession of aristocratic Southern presidents—Washington, Jefferson, Madison, and Monroe—was rapidly slipping into dim memory. And the Civil War, beginning in 1860, would finally sweep away what vestiges remained of the leisurely planter class that dominated the nation's early political life.

Even as early as the turbulent 1830s, the genteel tradition and the virtues of the country gentleman were fast giving way to the ideal of the rough-hewn frontiersman, the self-made man, personified by President Andrew Jackson. Jackson's presidency marked the granting of the vote to almost all white males. The "spoils system" was enthroned as a means of rewarding political loyalty. The factory and the marketplace—industry and commerce—were becoming the major influences in American life, as contrasted with Southern agrarianism.

In letters as well as in economics, the "Northern way" was destined to prevail until well into the twentieth century. But meanwhile Edgar Allan Poe could sincerely believe that it was only proper for one reared as he had been, as a Southern gentleman, to play a leading role in American culture. Unlike most Southern aristocrats, however, circumstances demanded that he fight tooth and claw for the recognition that other authors, through family connections, could claim without struggle.

On February 20, 1831, Poe arrived in New York City penniless and sick. With no place else to look for help, his thoughts again turned to the Allans. According to a letter he wrote home to Richmond at the time, he considered himself on his "death bed." Perhaps this was exaggerated, since within one week he recovered sufficiently to work alongside publisher Elam Bliss on the proofs for *Poems* (Second Edition).

The 124-page collection was printed on ordinary paper between pale-green covers. It was dedicated "To the U.S. Corps of Cadets." Most of the cadets were dismayed when they saw the book to find no humorous barbs at the academy's officers, and instead only serious, sometimes difficult poetry.

Convinced that his third book, like the earlier two, would net him little if any profit, Poe left New York for Baltimore intending to live with relatives. He arrived at the end of March 1831. By this time his grandmother Mrs. Poe was almost totally helpless with paralysis; and his brother Henry, seriously tubercular, was slipping toward death. Nevertheless Mrs. Clemm, with her usual motherly strength, insisted that "Eddie" remain in the household on Milk Street. There was room for him with Henry in the attic, she said, and then proceeded to stretch the already meager food budget to feed another mouth.

Edgar tried to obtain regular work, first as an editor, then as a schoolteacher. But he could not find a position. In August 1831, Henry died, leaving Edgar Poe deeply depressed and also in debt for Henry's doctor bills. By now he found it necessary to resort regularly to borrowing money from friends.

In his despondency Poe came to rely increasingly for emotional support on Mrs. Clemm. This unusual woman exercised as great an influence on Edgar's later life as John Allan had on his youth. Born in 1790, and therefore nearly twenty years older than Poe, Maria Poe Clemm was a younger sister of Edgar's father, David. She had married a widower with five children and had three children of her own by him before he, too, died. Only one child, nine-year-old Virginia Maria, Edgar's full cousin, still lived with her in 1831 when Edgar joined the family.

Virginia, whom Poe called "Sissy," was from all accounts a beautiful child. Slight, with a round face and deep blue-gray eyes, she is usually described in Poe family letters which have been preserved, as happy and highly intelligent. From the beginning she is said to have adored her flamboyant, charming cousin, "Eddie."

Hard pressed by poverty, Poe entered a short-story contest sponsored by the *Philadelphia Saturday Courier*, a newspaper. His story, *Metzengerstein*, did not win the prize but it was published in the *Courier*, which was encouraging, even if it did not put money on the table.

In November 1831, money matters suddenly took on a desperate cast when authorities notified

Edgar that he would be arrested for debt.* The amount, eighty dollars, seemed monumental to the wretchedly poor little family on Milk Street, Baltimore.

There was nowhere else for Edgar to turn but to John Allan; and faced with a possible term in debtor's prison he pleaded for help. "If you wish me to humble myself before you I am humble— Sickness and misery have left me not a shadow of pride . . . Do not let me perish for a sum of money which you would never miss." There was no answer. Mrs. Clemm sent a heartrending note of her own, confiding that she had been able to raise only twenty dollars. Finally, Allan sent money, but through an agent, without so much as a comment. Poe just barely avoided imprisonment, but the money was the last he was to receive from John Allan.

Even with his personal fortunes at low ebb, Poe found time for romance. This time it was an auburn-haired Baltimore neighbor, Mary Devereaux. He first noticed her while looking out the window of the attic where he wrote. The two began flirting by waving white handkerchief signals to each other. Edgar had Virginia Clemm carry notes for him. Eventually he requested and received a lock of Miss Devereaux's hair.

Handsome and poised, with an erect military

*It is not clear who brought charges against Poe, but it may well have been Sergeant "Bully" Graves.

61

bearing, Poe swept Mary Devereaux off her feet. The two became constant companions. She later wrote of him as "passionate in his love," but also "jealous," "intense," and incapable of controlling his feelings.

Once, after drinking champagne with some former cadet friends from West Point, Poe came to visit Mary. The alcohol had exercised its usual effect on him, and before long the two lovers quarreled on the front steps of the Devereaux home.

Mary stormed inside, slamming the door in Poe's face. When he tried to follow her, the girl's mother barred the way. Poe impulsively tried to push past the tall, sturdily built matron to reach Mary.

"I have a right!" he cried. "She is my wife now in the sight of Heaven!"

But Mrs. Devereaux refused. Edgar, furious, turned and left. Several days later, Mary's uncle wrote a biting letter to Poe condemning his conduct. Poe, livid with rage, returned and whipped the uncle—who was a man of over fifty—with a cowhide.

Inevitably the story became public. Poe's reputation grew as a man of violent temper, knowing no bounds in his sexual needs, and unable to control his emotions.

In June 1832, Edgar received word that John Allan was ill. But by the time he arrived in Richmond he found instead that his foster father was well and away at the office. There to greet the poet in what once had been his home was the new Mrs. Allan.

The two argued bitterly, Poe accusing the woman who had replaced his beloved "Ma" of marrying the Scotsman for his money; he even spoke harshly of the couple's infant son who was asleep upstairs. Mrs. Allan ordered Poe from the house. At first he refused to leave, but finally, with a characteristic flourish of bitter sarcasm on his lips, Poe departed.

By his visit to Richmond he had succeeded only in placing still more distance between himself and Allan. Any lingering thoughts of a legacy which he might have been harboring were now out of the question. He had no choice but to return to his attic in Baltimore and write.

And write he did. Thinking of himself, he later had one of his satiric story characters say, "How I labored—how I toiled—how I wrote! Ye Gods, did I *not* write? I knew not the word 'ease.' . . . Through good report and through ill report, I—wrote. Through sunshine and through moonshine I—wrote!"

For Edgar Allan Poe writing was a passion. It was also a grim necessity.

Despite all of his efforts Edgar discovered that he could not support himself on poetry alone.

Tired of depending on friends for loans and remembering his success with his first story, "Metzengerstein," he turned to fiction, for which there was a better market. One result was a series of eleven satiric stories called "The Tales of the Folio Club." These were pieces supposedly written by members of a pretentious literary club, meeting each time at the home of the member who, according to the group assembled at the last meeting, had written the worst story. The host for one session Poe describes is Mr. Rouge et Noir. Other members include Mr. Convulvulus Gondola, a traveler; De Rerum Natura, Esqr., a greenish-looking man enchanted with the outdoors; and Mr. Solomon Seadrift, who rather resembles a fish in appearance.

Poe's Folio Club stories, intended to be humorous, were sometimes so filled with exact detail—usually of morbid horror—that the satire was lost in realism. At first he had no success in publishing them. Then came the stroke of fortune he needed. In July 1833, the *Baltimore Sunday Visiter* announced a contest with a prize of fifty dollars for the best short story and twenty-five dollars for the best poem. Poe carefully recopied his best Folio .Club stories; he used the Roman manuscript letters that he had developed to make his handwriting look like printing.

In October the prizes were announced. One of Poe's stories, "MS. Found in a Bottle," won the short story award. His poem, "The Coliseum," would have taken the poetry prize, too, except that the judges refused to allow one author to win both awards.

Winning the prize was important to Poe because of the publicity he gained from it; there were few such awards at the time, and at last Edgar was receiving a share of attention in the literary world. After the story appeared in print he dressed in his best clothes and paid personal visits to the three contest judges, prominent men of Baltimore, to thank them for selecting his work.

One of the judges, John Latrobe, remembered Poe vividly, especially recalling the author's well modulated "almost rhythmical" voice, his high forehead, pale skin, erect bearing, and easy, quiet manner. "Coat, hat, boots, and gloves had evidently seen their best days," wrote Latrobe, "but so far as mending and brushing go, everything had been done apparently, to make them presentable. . . . On most men," continued Latrobe, "his clothes would have looked shabby and seedy, but there was something about this man that prevented one from criticizing his garments. . . . Gentleman was written all over him."

Another of the judges, John P. Kennedy, was also deeply impressed by Poe. The two became close friends, and it was Kennedy's patronage that first opened the way to Poe's literary success. Kennedy encouraged the poverty-stricken young writer to submit his "Tales of the Folio Club" to Carey, Lea & Carey for publication. He also persuaded the editors of *Godey's Lady's Book*, a mass-circulation magazine of the day, to accept one of the stories in the series.

In the spring of 1834, Poe abruptly stopped working and returned to Richmond. This time, he was informed, John Allan definitely was on his deathbed. After the author's last embarrassing visit to Allan House, the servants had been instructed to keep him out. But Edgar stormed past Mrs. Allan and brushed aside the servants to encounter his foster father face-to-face. Despite everything that had happened he still clung to some hope for a reconciliation. Perhaps he only wanted to pay his final respects. But Allan would have none of it. Grabbing the walking stick which was propped beside his bed, he raised himself from his pillows and ordered Edgar to leave the house at once. On March 27, 1834, Allan died. In his will he provided even for some of his illegitimate children. But for his foster son, Edgar Allan Poe, once his greatest pride, there was not a penny.

With John Allan dead, Poe, now twenty-five years old, came to regard the Clemm household as his true home. He looked to Mrs. Clemm as a mother, even calling her "Muddie," and she returned his affection. The twelve-year-old Virginia was still another factor. The two were full cousins, but having lived under the same roof together for four years they became closely tied to each other. Virginia was flattered by the attentions of her charming, gifted older cousin. Poe, on the other hand, found himself intrigued by Virginia's delicate body, blossoming into early womanhood; he always preferred thin, lithe women.

By the laws of most states in the nation, even today, the marriage of full cousins is prohibited. The idea of incest—sexual relations between close realtives—repelled Poe, but simultaneously attracted him. His interest found literary expression in the unusual story "Berenice," in which the hero experiences a haunting, maniacal love for his cousin.

Neilson Poe, another cousin, as well as other Baltimore relatives who occasionally contributed small amounts of money to the household, objected to the budding romance between Edgar and Virginia. But the relationship continued to grow. Mrs. Clemm, eager to tie Edgar to the household as a breadwinner, tacitly encouraged it.

Poe, already dependent on Mrs. Clemm, now came to rely on John P. Kennedy for emotional and financial support. Once Kennedy invited the writer to dinner. Having only his shabby clothes to wear, Poe swallowed his pride and answered in a note:

> Your kind invitation to dinner today has wounded me to the quick. I cannot come—and

for reasons of the most humiliating nature in my personal appearance.

With deep "mortification" Poe requested a loan of twenty dollars to buy a suit of clothes. Kennedy, at last aware of his protégé's truly desperate situation, provided him not only with money for clothes but food for the Clemms' table and the use of a horse for exercise.

More importantly, Kennedy introduced Poe to the editor of the *Southern Literary Messenger,* a literary magazine based in Richmond. At Kennedy's personal urging the *Messenger* accepted "Berenice," as well as regular book reviews and literary criticism by Poe. The five- and ten-dollar checks that began arriving kept the Clemms and Poe from starvation.

Thomas W. White, the editor of the *Messenger,* was sufficiently impressed with Poe's work to offer the impoverished writer a full-time job. Delighted at the prospect of drawing a regular paycheck, and also at returning "home" to Richmond, Poe agreed.

His departure was delayed by the death of his grandmother, Mrs. David Poe, on July 7, 1835. The burden of caring for a helpless invalid was over for Mrs. Clemm; but with Mrs. Poe's death her government pension checks stopped coming. At this time, too, Edgar experienced a period of illness, accompanied by deep depression. He began to develop symptoms that his doctor diagnosed as heart disease. He also was thoroughly exhausted by the emotional strains of the past years and his seemingly endless struggle against poverty.

Alcohol offered him some release, but an unsatisfactory one—as his experience at the University of Virginia and later at West Point demonstrated. Opium, he discovered, was more successful.* It gave him forgetfulness yet did not prevent him from working. Moreover, he was able to incorporate into his stories the intimate details of the drug's effects on him. Although he succeeded in restricting his intake of both stimulants, alcohol and opium, there is little doubt that he grew to depend on them regularly, especially as the general state of his health deteriorated. Alcohol in particular became his crutch in facing the world's realities.

In August 1835, Poe appeared once again on the streets of Richmond, the city of his boyhood. Still looking every inch the aristocrat in his all-black suit and black beaver hat, he was nonetheless a

---

*A controversy still rages among Poe scholars about whether or not he used drugs. There is no question that he purchased laudanum frequently; it was a drug containing opium available at the time across drugstore counters like aspirins today. During his many illnesses he is known to have begged for morphine. His intimate familiarity with the effects of drugs would be uncanny for a non-user. A better question perhaps is not *whether* Poe used drugs but *how often.*

different man. There was no way to conceal the haunting eyes and nervous glance that had grown upon him since the happy days when, as a favored child, he romped about the Allan household.

He came to Richmond alone, intending to send later for Virginia and Mrs. Clemm. For the first four weeks he was so feverishly busy with his work at the *Southern Literary Messenger* that he had little time to miss them. There were reviews to write, submissions by authors to evaluate, old friends from his childhood to visit.

But after this initial outburst of enthusiastic activity his spirits began to flag. He was hit by a severe case of melancholia, or deep depression (a little-understood condition so common that in recent years it has even afflicted a Democratic party vice-presidential nominee and an astronaut).

Desperately eager not to miss his chance for success Poe tried to snap out of his depression by using alcohol. One morning he arrived drunk at the *Messenger* office. Thomas White was furious. There was no room on his staff, he said, for an editor—no matter how brilliant—who had to drink before breakfast. Once again, Poe found himself without a job.

Sick and in disgrace, Poe returned to Baltimore on September 20. Two days later he took out a license to marry his cousin, Virginia Clemm, possibly hoping to assure at least some stability in his life. The two were secretly married at St. Paul's

Episcopal Church with no witnesses but Mrs. Clemm and the minister present. Edgar was twenty-six, Virginia thirteen. Probably at Poe's request no entry was made in the church register.*

Within days after the ceremony Poe wrote to his former employer, Thomas White, asking for another chance. White agreed, but with the express understanding that if Poe were ever again drunk the arrangement would be immediately dissolved. Reprieved, the gifted author left at once for Richmond.

Mrs. Clemm and Poe's child-wife Virginia followed him shortly afterward to the pleasant but cramped room he had rented for the family at Mrs. Yarrington's boardinghouse in downtown Richmond. The marriage to Virginia was kept secret and she was introduced as his cousin. Descriptions of her at the time speak of a "simple child," "sweet," with "gentle manners," and "small for her age." Like all the women Poe loved, she was pale and delicate, with a hint of death lingering about her.

Back in White's good graces, at least for the time, Poe worked with the frenzy of a man possessed. According to one tabulation, in a little more than fourteen months ending in December

*The "secret marriage" is characterized by Poe biographer A. H. Quinn as a figment of Maria Clemm's imagination, although she swore to it. Hervey Allen, a specialist on Poe, presents highly persuasive arguments for accepting the story.

1836, Poe produced for the *Messenger* eighty-three lengthy reviews, six poems, four essays, and three new short stories.

For each monthly issue of the magazine he turned out about twenty thousand words of copy—nearly the length of this book. In addition, he also handled all of the journal's correspondence and evaluated manuscripts submitted for publication. For this he initially received a salary of ten dollars a week—one dollar above the cost of food and lodging at Mrs. Yarrington's. But Poe was becoming known. His criticism, harsh yet scrupulously fair, drew widespread attention. His feature articles attracted new subscribers. As the circulation of the *Messenger* climbed from 500 readers to 2,000 and then to 3,500, White grudgingly advanced the salary of his remarkable editor by two dollars a week.

A two-dollar raise was modest indeed, compared with the flood of profits White now realized. But to Poe it was a sign of better times. He was encouraged, too, by a letter from Harper & Brothers urging him to submit a book-length story for publication. With such optimistic developments buoying his spirits he decided that the time was ripe to marry Virginia in a public ceremony, complete with wedding cake, ring, and guests.

The wedding was at Mrs. Yarrington's on May 16, 1836. Although Poe's "cousin" was still not quite fourteen, to avoid legal complications the marriage certificate listed her as "of the full age of twenty-one years." The wedding party included Mr. White and other staff members of the *Messenger,* Mrs. Yarrington, and several guests at the boardinghouse. Mrs. Clemm handled most of the arrangements herself.

After a two-week honeymoon at the home of a newspaper editor in Petersburg, the Poes returned to Richmond. Edgar soon found himself deeply involved with the magazine again. More relaxed, he allowed his output of critical material to slacken, but it was still the biting sharpness of his reviews that focused national attention on the little *Southern Literary Messenger.*

Poe's work as a critic was notable for its rigor and detail. Unlike most critics of the day, he insisted on a close textual analysis, sometimes considering a work line by line, with abundant examples and quotations. According to Poe, literary criticism should be limited to the individual work of art, not to such lesser matters as the historical background of the time or the personality of the author. Thus today's so-called "New Criticism" owes much to Poe's insistence on what he regarded as the cardinal principle of literary judgment: a focus directly on art, rather than on the artist. In that sense Poe was far ahead of his time.

He was noteworthy, too, as a critic in his capacity to separate the lasting from the transient. Before any other major critic, for example, he was able to write of Nathaniel Hawthorne's early work, *Twice-Told Tales*, that: "The style is purity itself. Force abounds. High imagination gleams from every page. Mr. Hawthorne is a man of truest genius."*

Twice Poe broke his resolution to stay away from alcohol. Both times his pleas for forgiveness convinced the fatherly Mr. White to soften and relent. Finally it was Edgar himself who determined to break with the magazine. The man-killing work schedule left him little time for his own creative writing. Only two installments were complete on his projected novel, *The Narrative of Arthur Gordon Pym*. Poe had arranged to have the work appear serially in the *Messenger* before its publication in book form. Impatient with his slow progress and restless to take the next step in his literary career, Poe delivered graceful farewell remarks in the January 1837 issue of the journal.

White, too, it appears was ready for a change. He had reached the limit of his patience over Poe's drinking. Futhermore, the brilliant, temperamental Poe could not resist a patronizing attitude toward White, the businessman-proprietor, who exercised the right of final decision in literary as well as financial matters.

With the experience at the *Messenger* behind him, Edgar Allan Poe set out for the North accom-

*Quoted by Robert Regan in his introduction to *Poe: A Collection of Critical Essays* (Englewood Cliffs, N.J.: Prentice-Hall, 1967), p. 3.

panied by his wife and his aunt. He was ready now, or so he thought, to establish a magazine of his own. And where was a more appropriate place to begin than the publishing capital of the nation, New York City?

# 5

## *dreams of gold, days of lead* (1837–1844)

Poe, often unfortunate in the risks he took, arrived in New York at just the wrong time. A few months after his departure from the *Messenger,* the nation was plunged into the most serious economic disorder it had experienced to that time—the "Panic of 1837."

President Andrew Jackson had systematically removed government deposits from the Bank of the United States, which he detested, and placed the money in "pet banks" throughout the country. These banks, in turn, had used the deposits as the basis for extending speculative credit to customers. Jackson, hoping to stem the tide of wild speculation which ensued, issued the Specie Circular requiring that all payments to the federal treasury had to be made in gold or silver. The result was a rash of bank failures and, before long, a full-scale depression.

Poe suffered greatly from the business collapse.

True, he was caught with very little paper currency. But many newspaper and magazine owners were. And as one after another of them closed his doors, he found himself increasingly destitute in New York City—unable to find employment or a market for his writings.

Mrs. Clemm, Virginia, and he finally settled in a rented house at 113½ Carmine Street in Greenwich Village. There they took in three or four borders, including William Cowans, a bookseller who introduced Poe to Washington Irving, William Cullen Bryant, and other prominent New York writers of the time.

Out of hunger and a continuing drive for recognition, Poe kept writing. One of his tales, "Von Jung, The Mystific," appeared in the *American Monthly Magazine*. He published another, "Siope—A Fable," in the *Baltimore Book*. He also did reviews for the *New York Review*, and in July 1838 his fourth book was published, *The Narrative of Arthur Gordon Pym*.

*Pym* is an episodic but highly graphic adventure tale, tied together by one paramount element—horror. Its hero is successively imprisoned without food in the hold of a ship, survives a bloody mutiny, and then is set adrift at sea in an open boat. He and his companions in the boat, close to death, draw lots to see which will die to provide food for the others. The winners kill the unlucky loser and, over several days, eat him piece by piece and drink his blood. In the course of the book there are scenes of gruesome terror, recounted in memorable detail: incidents of live burial; of carrion birds casually dipping their blood-drenched beaks into the chests of dead crewmen on a ship drifting aimlessly after all aboard have died of plague; of a ghastly all-white Antarctic landscape engulfing Pym as he comes face-to-face at the book's conclusion with "a shrouded human figure, very far larger in its proportions than any dweller among men. And the hue of the skin was of the perfect whiteness of the snow."

The eerie tale, artistically complete in its powerful mood of the macabre, failed even to sell out the copies in its first edition. In the summer of 1838, with no money to pay the rent or buy food for the table, Poe and his family left New York for Philadelphia. They barely managed to scrape together train fare for the journey.

The move was not a surrender, only a tactical retreat. As a publishing center Philadelphia closely rivaled New York. Some of the finest printers and engravers in the country were working there. Poe, moreover, had several literary friends in the city who could be expected to help him. He now began to investigate seriously the establishment of a national magazine under his own editorship.

The family lived in a succession of boarding-houses: at Twelfth Street near Arch, at 127 Arch

Street, at the corner of Sixteenth and Locust streets, and at a dwelling somewhere on Coates Street. Inability to pay the rent must have been as great a spur for the frequent moves as Poe's restlessness.

Philadelphia of that day was generally a prosperous city, the old brick houses laid out in neat rows, each house with its own water pump in front. Food was in good supply and low in price. Philadelphia suffered much less than New York from the effects of the Panic of 1837. Soon Poe became so busy that he even had to decline an offer to review a new book by Washington Irving.

One project he was working on was a school textbook about shells, published under his name in 1839 as *The Conchologist's First Book: or, A System of Testaceous Malacology*. In actual fact, Poe only wrote the preface to the book. He translated some sections from a French source and lifted whole segments verbatim from a British account by Thomas Brown, without troubling to credit his source. Piracy, particularly in the preparation of school textbooks, was common practice at the time, since international copyright regulations were in a state of chaos. But Poe's actions quite properly brought a torrent of literary abuse down on him. All he ever realized for his trouble was a fee of fifty dollars paid for the use of his name as author by the book's sponsor, Thomas Wyatt, a Philadelphia neighbor.

Of profounder significance than such hack writing were the poems and stories that Poe began to produce in Philadelphia. One poem, "The Haunted Palace," almost certainly reflected Poe's mounting uneasiness about his own sanity; he was concerned about the "palace" of his mind. An important short story, "The Fall of the House of Usher" (1839), was also clearly autobiographical. It dealt with incestuous love—as in Poe's marriage to his cousin Virginia—and a woman's slowly wasting away to death—as in Virginia's declining health, which Poe was beginning to notice with alarm. Usher, like Poe, was a person of sensitivity and learning but weak, and incapable of stopping his own personal disintegration.

In May 1839, Poe won a job as coeditor of *Burton's Gentleman's Magazine.* His employer was William Evans Burton, known as "Bully Burton," a jovial English comedian and showman who had come to live in Philadelphia and turned to editing and publishing as a sideline. Poe livened the dreary pages of the "Gent's Mag," as he disdainfully called it, with such masterpieces as his stories "William Wilson," "Morella," "Ligeia," and "The Fall of the House of Usher." He produced in serial form "The Journal of Julius Rodman." But most importantly, at the age of thirty he succeeded in publishing his sixth book, a two-volume collection of stories, *Tales of the Grotesque and Arabesque.* Here were twenty-four pieces, among them some of Poe's finest tales. Yet public response was slight.

Meanwhile, Poe was having problems in his personal relationship with "Bully" Burton. Once again he was in danger of losing a job.

This time Poe had not been drinking. Deadly earnest and driven to high standards in his own writing and criticism, he was irritated by the light-hearted clumsiness of Burton, whom he came to regard as "the London buffoon." To Poe, the *Gentleman's Magazine* seemed trivial and shoddy. Burton, like Thomas White of the *Southern Literary Messenger,* insisted on his right to cast his own journal in whatever image he chose, not necessarily that of his haughty editor. He was particularly eager for Poe to tone down his harsh reviews and to avoid such controversial subjects as slavery.

The two men argued bitterly and then were reconciled. But Poe still openly flaunted the notion of starting a mass-circulation magazine of his own, based on the highest possible graphic and literary standards. As in his own prose and poetry he expected to make no compromise with excellence, regardless of the cost.

In May 1840, there was another clash. This time Poe resigned. Within five months Burton, far more interested in his theatrical connections than in the magazine, put his journal up for sale.

The purchaser was George Rex Graham, a lawyer who had been an editor of the *Saturday Evening Post* and owner of another magazine, the *Casket*. He paid Burton $3,500 for the *Gentleman's Magazine*—a dollar for each of the journal's 3,500 subscribers at the time. This he combined with the 1,500 subscribers to the *Casket* for a base of 5,000 readers. With Edgar Allan Poe as his editor the magazine skyrocketed in a little more than a year to a subscriber list of 37,000—to that date the largest in the world for a monthly magazine.

Poe had agreed to edit the new *Graham's Lady's and Gentleman's Magazine* with considerable reluctance. He felt fairly confident of finding financial backers and subscribers for his own projected *Penn Magazine*. But Graham was persuasive. He apparently promised Poe a salary increase after six months; also he expressed a willingness either to make him a partner in the new *Graham's* later or perhaps to help him start his own journal. These verbal promises, no matter how lacking in legal safeguards, were enough to convince Poe to postpone his plans for launching the *Penn Magazine;* the prospect of a steady income was too much for him to resist.

Graham paid his contributors well. Henry Wadsworth Longfellow received as much as fifty dollars for a poem; James Fenimore Cooper $1,800 for a story. Sometimes there were elaborate fashion engravings costing $200 a plate. But it was Poe whose elevated pages of literary criticism and correspondence with well known authors made the magazine's phenomenal financial success possible. And for him there was the modest reward of $800 per year in salary and a small page rate on his contributions. Customarily, editors of the day were paid $1,500 or even $2,000 a year. Graham's promise of a larger salary never materialized; nor did the hope of a share in the magazine's profits.

Still, Poe was rewarded in other ways. He was practically the unchallenged ruler of the outstanding mass-circulation magazine in America. He corresponded regularly and at length with Irving, Cooper, Lowell, Longfellow—the literary giants of his day. In the *Graham's* offices he was consulted, deferred to, praised—all of which he needed. In the nation at large he developed a reputation for brilliance and originality. Graham himself was delighted to have Poe as his editor. And why not? On an investment of $3,500 the magazine was soon grossing approximately $100,000 or more per year, of which he could personally expect a yearly return of about $30,000, a great sum of money in those days.

According to Graham, Poe cared little for money, turning his monthly checks over to Mrs. Clemm. Aside from his craft, the magazine owner recalled, writing in 1850, Poe's love was entirely for his wife Virginia. It was:

a sort of rapturous worship of the spirit of beauty which he felt was fading before his eyes. I have seen him hovering around her when she was ill, with all the fond fear and tender anxiety of a mother for her first born—her slightest cough causing in him a shudder, a breast chill that was visible.

The frail health of "Sissy" must have been one important reason that Poe was, in fact, intensely concerned with money, contrary to his employer's loftily detached judgment. In his years as an editor of *Graham's Magazine* Poe tried hard to obtain a job with the federal government. Half hoping for a patronage appointment, he had taken time from his literary labors during the Election of 1840 to work on behalf of William Henry Harrison, the Whig party's successful candidate for the presidency.

But the fates, as usual, were cruel to Poe. Only one month after taking office the aged Harrison died, bringing Vice-President John Tyler to power. Lacking political influence, Poe wrote to a friend in Washington to help him:

I would be glad to get almost any appointment, even a $500.00 one, so that I have something independent of letters for a subsistence. To coin one's brain into silver, at the nod of a master, is, to my thinking, the hardest task in the world. . . .

84

The appointment, however, did not come, and removed by only one step from poverty Poe continued month after month to "coin his brain into silver." In rapid succession he produced "The Murders in the Rue Morgue," "The Mystery of Marie Rogêt," and "The Gold Bug."

These, like his earlier tales, were replete with brutality, murder, sadism, burial before death, and other abominations. But there was a difference. For they are stories in which the heroes are persons of almost perfect logic. Rational human beings marshal their intelligence to solve insoluble murders, trap criminals with their superior brains, uncover buried pirate treasure, and break elaborate secret codes. It was an age of romanticism—fond of stories filled with fog-shrouded landscapes, crumbling castles, clanking chains, helpless maidens in distress. Sentiment, intuition, emotion, and feeling were highly prized; thought and reason were not. Yet Poe introduced the reasoned, logical "detective story" and made it popular with the reading public. He, more than anyone else, deserves to be called the father of that particular form of short story. It has changed little since he perfected it.

Using the same rational techniques, Poe had the audacity to predict the outcome of a Charles Dickens story which in 1841 was appearing serially in America. Learning of the feat, Dickens declared of Poe that "the man must be the devil."

When the great British author visited the United States in 1842 he had two long meetings with Poe. The two discussed the lamentable state of international copyright law. The matter was of more than academic interest to Poe, since in the absence of adequate copyright regulations, American publishing firms competed savagely to pirate British books rather than seek out American authors—to whom they would have had to pay royalties. Dickens promised to try to get Poe's books published in England, but he did not succeed.

Poe, at the age of thirty-two, was now at the height of his creative powers. He was a person of renown in American letters. And, through the frugality of Mrs. Clemm, there were even a few luxuries in the household—some painted chairs, a few rugs, a small piano, and a harp for Virginia. True, George Rex Graham had not lived up to his word and shared the profits which Poe's hard work and genius had created. But the dream of owning his own magazine, now referred to as *The Stylus*, still burned brightly for Poe, as the year 1841 drew to a close.

The month of January 1842 had not ended when tragedy struck. Virginia, dressed all in white, was playing her harp and singing before a small group of friends and relatives at the Poe home on Coates Street. Her voice, as always clear and beautiful, rose for a particularly high note. Suddenly she gagged and clutched at her throat. A stream of blood gushed forth, spilling over the white of her dress.

Edgar rushed for the doctor. There was no doubt, it was tuberculosis, in its advanced state. Edgar's child-wife might linger on, even for several years, but death at an early age was certain.

Virginia recovered partially only to repeat the scene of the gushing blood again and again. Her face grew waxen, her eyes liquid and lustrous. Frantic, Poe turned to his usual escape, drink. Sometimes he would be away from his office for several days. Graham no longer could count on him. He brought in other editors to help put out the magazine.

One day Edgar returned to the offices of *Graham's* to find another editor seated at his desk. It was the Reverend Dr. Rufus Wilmot Griswold, a poetry anthologist whose work Poe had once maliciously panned. Graham half-heartedly tried to persuade Poe to stay on but, proud, Poe refused. Deeply resenting his treatment by Graham, he left the building resolving never to return.

Now his drinking increased. He went off on a wild binge, appearing in Jersey City at the home of the red-headed Mary Devereaux, for whom in Baltimore he once had shown such passionate love. He traced her in New York City through her husband's name. Then, losing the address the husband had given him, inquired crazily about her whereabouts among passengers riding the ferry-boat to Jersey City. A crewman knew her. Finally, his eyes by then out of focus from drinking, he arrived at her door. Mary, happily married, did not know what to think of his strange behavior. Several days later a party of searchers led by Mrs. Clemm, who in great anxiety had followed after him, discovered Poe wandering half-mad in the woods outside of Jersey City. Meanwhile, Virginia, desperately ill in Philadelphia, had been frantic with worry over his absence.

Shortly afterward Poe moved his unhappy family to a cottage near Spring Garden Street, which later was maintained as a memorial to him. The cottage, with its pear trees and pleasant garden, might have been the setting for a poetic idyll. But it was not. Virginia's health continued to deteriorate; although still smiling and cheerful she suffered attack after attack. Edgar, heartsick at his wife's illness and deprived of a steady income at *Graham's*, was stricken with a nervous collapse. Melancholy and depression closed in on him, and he retreated deeper into drink. Often Mrs. Clemm followed his path from tavern to tavern until she found him and brought him home. During the summer of 1842 he wrote scarcely a line.

Briefly Poe renewed his efforts to obtain a government job and to gain backing for his proposed magazine, *The Stylus*. The two projects became tied together in negotiations with Thomas C.

88

Clarke, a prosperous Philadelphia publisher. Clarke went so far as to sign agreements for starting the journal with Poe and an outstanding illustrator. Clarke then dispatched Poe to Washington to obtain subscriptions for *The Stylus* among prominent government officials. It seemed a reasonable assignment. Poe had once published a highly favorable review of poetry by Robert Tyler, the President's son, and through that connection even succeeded in scheduling an interview with President Tyler himself.

As usual on important occasions Poe worked himself into a high state of nervous excitement. His host in Washington, J. E. "Rowdy" Dow, insisted that he relax with a glass of port wine. It took only a glass or two before the damage was done. By the next morning Poe had spent all of the expense money Clarke had given him and even had to request credit for a shave at a local barber shop.

By Poe's judgment he created *"a sensation"* in the government offices, soliciting subscriptions. But given his drunken state it was not a "sensation" calculated to inspire confidence. Robert Tyler canceled the interview with his father rather than risk Poe's making a poor impression. He also canceled a lecture that Poe had been scheduled to give. Poe's friends put him on a train for Philadelphia babbling wildly, his black Spanish cloak wrapped tightly around him to ward off the chills of his "recovery." Dow notified Mrs. Clemm to meet Poe at the train station, which, dutifully, she did.

The trip to Washington had been an unqualified disaster. With it, Poe's prospective nomination for a job in the Philadelphia Customs House evaporated. He had demonstrated again that he needed some kind of stimulant, especially in a crisis situation, and that the stimulant produced in him greater problems than it cured. He had ruined what remained of his reputation. And now, to crown Poe's disgrace, the cautious Mr. Clarke withdrew his offer to back *The Stylus*. The magazine—Poe's fondest dream—was dead.

Sick and discouraged, he was reduced to writing to Rufus Griswold, the editor who had taken his place at *Graham's,* for a loan of five dollars. Griswold, thinly masking his pleasure at the misfortune of the reviewer who once had ridiculed his poetry anthology, sent a check.

Poe's lone triumph in the year 1843 was the award of a one-hundred-dollar prize for his short story, "The Gold Bug." The story appeared in two installments (June 21 and 28) in the *Dollar Newspaper,* which had sponsored the contest. Eventually it became the most frequently reprinted of any of Poe's stories. For its realistic setting and details Poe dredged his memory, recalling vividly his days on the beach at Sullivan's Island when he was serving in the army.

The prize money came when his personal fortunes and literary career were at their lowest ebb. To the desolate writer, the check must have seemed almost like a gift from heaven. According to one observer, it was at this time that Poe used to walk the streets:

> in madness or in melancholy, with lips moving in indistinct curses, or with eyes upturned in passionate prayers (never for himself, for he felt, or professed to feel, that he was already damned), but for their happiness who were at the moment the objects of his [concern]. . . . [Mrs. Clemm and Virginia].

Besides "The Gold Bug" one other famous work was begun during this period of anguish in Poe's life—his poem "The Raven." He had first developed the idea for the poem from a reference to the ominous bird in Dickens's story, *Barnaby Rudge.* After working on the project from time to time over almost two years, he presented himself at the offices of *Graham's Magazine,* hoping to sell it to his old employer. Graham would not buy the poem, but when Poe insisted on its virtues Graham called together his entire staff to give their opinions. They agreed with his judgment. The poverty-stricken Poe, however, pleaded his desperate need for money so earnestly that the hat was passed and fifteen dollars raised for Virginia and Mrs. Clemm. Familiar with their former colleague's personal habits, the staff insisted on turning the money over to Mrs. Clemm directly. Poe profited from the adverse criticism of "The Raven" by the magazine's staff and patiently continued to polish the work.

Earlier in his stay in Philadelphia Poe had produced three of his most memorable stories: "The Tell-Tale Heart," "The Pit and the Pendulum," and "The Black Cat." All are tales of morbid horror, replete with sadism. "The Black Cat" is typical. In it, the narrator tells how in a moment of passion, stimulated by alcohol, he cut out the eye of his pet cat and later hanged the animal.

> I hung it because . . . I knew that in so doing I was committing a sin—a deadly sin that would so jeopardize my immortal soul as to place it—if such a thing were possible—even beyond the reach of the infinite mercy of the Most Merciful and Terrible God.

Obsessed by guilt he brings home another black cat. Eventually he becomes enraged with this cat, too, and tries to kill it with an axe. When his wife tries to stop him he kills her instead and walls her body in the basement of his house. Police investigators, unable to find a corpse, are about to leave when the narrator, swelling with pride over his cleverness, taps the wall with his cane. A piercing shriek from behind the plaster panel reveals the secret of the horrible murder; he had accidentally walled in the cat, alive, with the body of his wife.

By the spring of 1844, at the age of thirty-five, Poe had little creative energy to expend on stories or poetry. He was reduced to nostalgic pieces about his youth in Virginia, such as "A Tale of the Ragged Mountains." By now, too, literary circles in the city buzzed over his drinking and his irresponsibility. Prospective financial backers for *The Stylus* wanted no part of a man of his reputation. "Sissy" meanwhile continued to cough out her life, still deprived of the good food and healthful climate so essential in treating tuberculosis.

Leaving Mrs. Clemm to sell the few family possessions which had not already been pawned, Poe bundled his fragile wife in warm clothing for a move to the only place where he thought there was still a chance for him to succeed—New York City.

The hopelessly forlorn couple arrived in Manhattan on April 6, 1844, drenched to the skin in a driving rainstorm. Poe spent twenty-five cents for an umbrella and also bought some thread for Virginia to mend his pants, which he had torn on a nail. In a life so unrelieved by humor as was Poe's there is welcome relief in the picture of the fearful spinner of horror tales seated on the bed without his trousers while his wife completes repairs.

As Poe wrote the next morning to "My Dear Muddie," Virginia missed her very much during that first night in New York, and "had a hearty cry ... because you and Caterina [the family's black cat] were not here." Train fare for Mrs. Clemm from Philadelphia would have been three dollars, and Poe did not have it to spare, even for the mainstay of the household.

The seven-dollar-a-week rooming house that he found on Greenwich Street "looked old and buggy," he told Mrs. Clemm, but it served "elegant" meals, he said. To the almost literally starving writer and his delicate wife, that was a point worth mentioning.

After finishing his letter to "Muddie," Poe set out bravely to face New York City's journalistic jungle, hopeful of reversing his woeful luck. In his pocket was all the money he had in the world, exactly four dollars and fifty cents. But, as usual, Poe's confidence in himself was boundless.

# 6

## *a bittersweet taste of fame*
## (1844–1847)

Poe burst upon the New York scene with the flamboyance of an 1844 Fourth of July fireworks display. He did it by selling to the *New York Sun*—a sensational, mass-circulation penny newspaper—the manuscript for "The Balloon Hoax." On April 13 the *Sun* featured the "Astounding News!" that a balloon piloted by Mr. Monck Mason had crossed the Atlantic in three days and landed at Sullivan's Island, South Carolina.

New Yorkers by the hundreds rushed to the offices of the *Sun*, blocking the entrance to the building—clamoring for copies of the "Extra" edition that was promised. Scalpers sold single copies for as much as half a dollar to people eager to read the exciting news.

Even after the hoax was discovered Poe could scarcely hide his satisfaction. He held the great mass of people in contempt, considering most of humanity his inferiors; thus he reveled in this

95

latest evidence of the "mobocracy's" stupidity. Popular rule, he thought, went hand in hand with the decline of American civilization.

In the 1840s Poe was almost alone in railing at the ostentatious architecture and greed for profit that characterized life in Manhattan. A Southern gentleman, albeit an impoverished one, he stood aghast to see the values and high idealism of the early Republic crumbling around him. The very landscape was being marred by ugliness. And he felt helpless to stop the nation's disintegration, as he felt helpless to stop his own personal decline.

In the hot summer of 1844, the Poes moved to the country for Virginia's health (accompanied by Mrs. Clemm, who had joined them about a week after their arrival in New York). They boarded on the Brennan farm, 216 acres with a rambling farmhouse at what is today Broadway and Eighty-fourth Street. The Brennans' food was excellent and the view of the nearby Hudson pleasing. At what is now Ninety-sixth Street a small stream entered the river, emerging from woodland, and it was here that passengers gathered from other farms to board the steamboat for Wall Street or for points farther up the river. Altogether the setting was charming and provided a lovely escape from the poverty dogging Poe's household.

"Eddie" and "Sissy" had immaculately clean rooms in the attic, just beneath the steeply sloping farmhouse roof, while "Muddie" had a spacious room on the first floor. For his study Poe chose a quaintly furnished room with a broad mantelpiece. The objects of that room, including a bust of Pallas Athena, soon would find their way into revisions of the most popular of all of his poems— "The Raven."

Although Poe worked painstakingly at polishing the poem throughout the summer, Mrs. Clemm observed his "hermit-like" existence on the Brennan farm with dismay, since no money was coming in. Finally she acted on her own, begging work for him from Nathaniel P. Willis, owner of the *New York Mirror*. The tender-hearted Willis could not refuse her pleas; it was in the pages of his weekly journal, therefore, that "The Raven" first appeared under Poe's signature, on February 8, 1845. Poe had inserted an earlier unsigned version in the *Mirror* on January 29 in order to stimulate interest in the identity of the author. Its first major exposure came in the *American Review* for February 1845.

With the publication of "The Raven," Edgar Allan Poe became famous overnight. Autograph hunters sought him out. British journals praised him. The poem was reprinted in newspapers across the United States. Swiftly it became almost universally known.

What were the reasons for its great popular success? Undoubtedly there was contemporary appeal in the theme: a symbolic bird entering the room of a lover sentimentally mourning his dead sweetheart, "Lenore." It was a time in American social history when sentiment and melancholy were highly prized. But more important perhaps in the poem's enduring popularity is its rhythmic, musical qualities and the repetition of the raven's haunting cry, "Nevermore . . ."

The memorable first stanza sets the work's bleak tone:

> Once upon a midnight dreary, while I
>     pondered, weak and weary,
> Over many a quaint and curious volume of
>     forgotten lore—
> While I nodded, nearly napping, suddenly
>     there came a tapping,
> As of some one gently rapping, rapping at my
>     chamber door.
> " 'Tis some visitor," I muttered, "tapping at my
>     chamber door—
>         Only this and nothing more."

As stanza follows stanza, the lover works himself into an emotional frenzy, knowing that he will "nevermore" be able to forget his lost Lenore. In despair he asks the bird whether he will ever again see Lenore:

> "Prophet!" said I, "thing of evil!—prophet still,
>     if bird or devil!

By that heaven that bends above us—by that
  God we both adore—
Tell this soul with sorrow laden if, within the
  distant Aidenn,
It shall clasp a sainted maiden whom the angels
  name Lenore—
Clasp a rare and radiant maiden whom the
  angels name Lenore."
            Quoth the Raven, "Nevermore."


At last the lover realizes that his haunting memories will be with him always, as the poem closes with two unforgettable stanzas:

"Be that word or sign of parting, bird or fiend!"
  I shrieked, upstarting—
"Get thee back into the tempest and the Night's
  Plutonian shore!
Leave no black plume as a token of that lie thy
  soul hath spoken!
Leave my loneliness unbroken!—quit the bust
  above my door!
Take thy beak from out my heart, and take thy
  form from off my door!"
            Quoth the Raven, "Nevermore."


And the Raven, never flitting, still is sitting, still
  is sitting
On the pallid bust of Pallas just above my
  chamber door;

And his eyes have all the seeming of a demon's
    that is dreaming,
And the lamp-light o'er him streaming throws
    his shadow on the floor;
And my soul from out that shadow that lies
    floating on the floor
                Shall be lifted—nevermore!

Whatever the reasons for the poem's success it
had, in Poe's words, "a great run," (great popularity)

> but I wrote it for the express purpose of run-
> ning—just as I did the "Gold Bug", you know.
> The bird beat the bug, though, all hollow.

Few poems in the English language have been
recited more often to audiences. Poe himself
became known across the country as "The Rav-
en."
    If "The Raven" made Poe famous it did not
make him rich. He sold the rights to it for ten
dollars. Yet fame, for him, was a matter of considerable importance. As he once declared with
uncharacteristic openness:

> I love fame—I dote on it—I idolize it—I would
> drink to the very dregs the glorious intoxica-
> tion. I would have incense ascend in my hon-
> our from every hill and hamlet, from every
> town and city on this earth. Fame! Glory!—

they are life-giving breath, and living blood. No man lives, unless he is famous!

Another spur to Poe's growing fame was a detailed biographical sketch of his life written for *Graham's Magazine* by the renowned American poet James Russell Lowell. N. P. Willis reprinted Lowell's article in the *New York Mirror*, bringing Poe's name into even greater prominence. In England Elizabeth Barrett Browning expressed appreciation for his work, as he had previously done for hers.

At last Poe was winning the literary respect for which he had sacrificed so much. In February 1845, partly through Lowell's influence, he became a partner in the *Broadway Journal*, a new weekly literary magazine sponsored by John Bosco and Charles F. Briggs. In exchange for editorial work and a page of original copy per week he was to receive one-third of the journal's profits. Although not quite the realization of his dream for *The Stylus*, it was a splendid opportunity. To be closer to his work Poe moved Virginia and Mrs. Clemm once again, this time to a comfortable rooming house on Amity Street in Greenwich Village.

Even before becoming editor of the *Broadway Journal*, Poe had written for that journal a series of attacks on the poetry of Henry Wadsworth Longfellow, particularly the New England poet's anthology, *The Waif*. Longfellow's reverent supporters rushed to his defense, while their idol maintained a discreet and sensible silence.

For five weeks the "Little Longfellow War" raged in earnest. Heated charges filled the air, serving to stimulate public interest and increase sales of the *Broadway Journal*. The only real loser in the affair was Poe's reputation. At first he had stated a moderate argument, that Longfellow, a gifted poet, was currying popular favor with what for him was inferior verse. But as the conflict escalated in intensity Poe threw about largely unfounded charges of plagiarism at his renowned rival.

While the tumult over the "Little Longfellow War" gradually subsided, Poe worked fourteen or fifteen hours a day at his writing. He produced articles for *Godey's Lady's Book*, for *Graham's Magazine*, and for the *American Review*. He lectured and recited poetry, often to enthusiastic audiences. He wrote literary criticism.

In 1845 alone, two new volumes of his works appeared: *Tales by Edgar A. Poe* and *The Raven and Other Poems*. *Tales* contained twelve of his most popular stories: "The Gold Bug," "The Black Cat," "The Fall of the House of Usher," and others, selected and edited by Evert A. Duyckinck of Wiley & Putnam. The same publishing house presented *The Raven and other Poems,* described by one scholar today as "the most important volume of poetry that had been issued up until that time in America."*

Perhaps Poe was working too hard; perhaps he was concerned about Virginia's deteriorating condition. But once again he turned to drink, this time even more heavily than before. He was now at the height of his contemporary fame, lionized by the public, a welcome guest at the homes of New York's artistic élite. He was especially sought after by the city's literary hostesses. With his wife dying, Poe gradually began to seek emotional release and comfort in friendships with other women.

The first of those friendships was with Mrs. Frances Sargent Osgood, a poet married to the American painter Samuel S. Osgood. Poe praised her work in the pages of the *Broadway Journal,* and published verses "To F . . ." in her honor. There was intimate correspondence, letters saved both by Poe and Mrs. Osgood. Before long a public scandal erupted, exaggerated by the fact that the Reverend Dr. Rufus Griswold was also competing for the favors of the exciting Mrs. Osgood.

Charles Briggs now withdrew from the *Broadway Journal.* He had been offended by Poe's

*Hervey Allen, *Israfel: The Life and Times of Edgar Allan Poe* (New York: Farrar & Rinehart, 1934), p. 533.

drinking, by his conduct with Frances Osgood, and by the contempt Poe enjoyed showing in his personal conversation for the Bible and organized religion—sacrosanct topics at the time. Poe managed to borrow enough money to buy ownership of the journal. But ill from drinking and its effect on his delicate nervous system, he found himself too weak to work. Still he was well enough to follow Mrs. Osgood to Albany, where she and her husband had gone to live. He also was attracted to Mrs. Sarah Helen Whitman, another poet. Poe first saw Mrs. Whitman by moonlight in a rose garden; later he learned that her name was "Helen." For the romantic Poe, that was enough. From a distance, never having met her, he fell madly in love with her.

Meanwhile, with the breakdown in his health his literary fortunes began to crumble. He had gone deeply into debt to buy the *Broadway Journal* and could not pay the notes when they came due. The magazine's circulation was dropping. And Poe succeeded in filling its pages only by publishing and republishing his old works; he was too physically drained to create new ones.

Despondent, Poe went on a drunken spree. One final issue of the *Broadway Journal* appeared on January 3, 1846, and then the magazine folded. Poe had been unable to build the circulation of his own journal, as he had done with spectacular success before, for others.

Even after the demise of the *Broadway Journal* Poe continued to be seen in New York's literary circles. One contemporary female commentator noted that:

> His slender form, intellectual face and weird expression of eye never failed to arrest the attention of even the least observant. He did not affect the society of men, rather that of highly intellectual women with whom he liked to fall into a sort of eloquent monologue, half dream, half poetry. Men were intolerant of all this, but women fell under his fascination and listened in silence. . . .

Without work, caught up in deepening despair over Virginia's condition, Poe tried to make practical use of his contacts with other artists. Beginning in the spring of 1846, he published in the pages of *Godey's Lady's Book* a series of articles on the literary figures of New York. These sketches, which came to be known as *The Literati*, were highly controversial. Not all of Poe's judgments were negative, but enough important persons were offended that Poe found himself the object of violent counterattacks.

One of those who felt flagrantly abused was playwright and former editor, Thomas Dunn English, referred to by Poe as "Thomas Done Brown." Poe had written:

Mr. Brown had, for the motto on his magazine
cover, the words of Richelieu—

> . . . Men call me cruel,
> I am not:—I am *just*.

Here the two monosyllables "an ass"
should have been appended.

Poe even poked fun at English's spelling and
grammatical usage.

A principal result of the appearance of *The Literati* was a period of vicious, petty literary bickering with Poe at its center.

Poe tried to escape into seclusion by moving
Virginia and Mrs. Clemm to Turtle Bay on a farm
along the East River, at today's Forty-seventh
Street. There he hoped to spend as much time as
possible with Virginia while she passed through
the final stages of her illness and also to regain
control of his own faculties; he thought he was fast
approaching madness.

But even Turtle Bay was too close to the bustle
of the city and visits from inquisitive friends. In
May 1846, the Poe household removed to a small
cottage at Fordham, in what today is a blighted
area of high population in the Bronx but then was
only a coach stop on the stagecoach route northward from New York. Here at last, hoped Poe,
would be solitude.

Controversy, however, followed him even to
Fordham. First there was a scandal over Mrs.
Osgood's letters to Poe, some of which Mrs.

Clemm unwisely read to a visitor to the Fordham cottage. Poe returned the letters to Mrs. Osgood with abject apologies, but the relationship was finished. He also returned the letters of Mrs. Elizabeth Lummis Ellet, another lady with whom he had been in correspondence. But when Mrs. Ellet denied ever receiving the letters back her brother threatened Poe with a possible duel.

No sooner had that incident been cleared up—but not the malicious gossip surrounding it—than Thomas Dunn English let loose a double-barreled blast at Poe in the pages of the *New York Mirror*, accusing the poet of lying and forgery. This time Poe was so exasperated that he sued English for libel. In February 1847, the case came to trial, and Poe was awarded $492 in damages, of which after legal fees he retained $225.

But the damage to Poe's reputation by having his dirty linen washed in public was irreparable. His drinking, his problems with women, his poverty were now matters of public knowledge. Every day he received crank letters—many of them read by the dying Virginia—cruelly attacking him for his moral crimes, real and imaginary. Largely from this period came the image of Poe as a drunken ne'er-do-well.

In the lovely pastoral simplicity of Fordham, Poe and his little family sank into deep despair and hopeless poverty. "Muddie" gathered dandelion greens in the fields to make salads for her two sick "children"; during the fall of 1846 she was their only salvation. Poe was even too ill to accept a lucrative speaking engagement at the University of Vermont. He did almost no writing, only routine correspondence.

With the coming of winter the family's condition worsened. Virginia was now unable to leave her bed, with its pitiful mattress of straw. Her only cover was Poe's old West Point overcoat; she clutched Caterina the cat close to her body for a little extra warmth.

When word of the Poes' distress finally reached New York's literary circles one woman, Mrs. Marie Louise Shew, acted swiftly to help. Mrs. Shew was a New York City socialite, intensely interested in literary affairs. She arranged to have a feather bed sent to Virginia. Then, organizing a collection, she was able to present Mrs. Clemm with sixty dollars in cash. The kindly editor, N. P. Willis, used the pages of his magazine, the *Home Journal*, to print a moving appeal for money to help Poe and his family. The public's response was wholehearted, and as Virginia sank closer to death she was at least warm and well fed. Poe, though still proud, accepted the charity and wrote gracious letters of thanks to those who helped his wife in her last days.

Virginia continued to be sweet, smiling, and innocently tolerant of Edgar Allan Poe's many weaknesses. At the end of January 1847, Mary

Devereaux, Poe's old flame from his Baltimore days and still a close friend of Virginia's and Mrs. Clemm's, came to pay her last respects. Virginia surely must have remembered delivering Poe's love notes to Mary as a little girl.

According to Mary Devereaux's account, Virginia was placed in a large armchair with Poe beside her. "I had my hand in hers," wrote Mary,

> and she took it and placed it in Mr. Poe's, saying "Mary, be a friend to Eddie, and don't forsake him; he always loved you—didn't you, Eddie?"

Her body racked by pain, the pale, undernourished Virginia selflessly considered what would happen to her lonely husband, "Eddie," after her death.

On January 30, 1847, Mrs. Shew arrived at Fordham in answer to Poe's urgent request. Virginia took a picture of Poe from under her pillow and gave it to Mrs. Shew for safekeeping, along with a jewel box which he long had treasured. It had once belonged to Poe's mother. She also read aloud two letters that she said would clear Poe of any wrongdoing in his relationship with John Allan, his foster father. The two letters have never been recovered.

That night, in great pain, Virginia Clemm Poe died. She was twenty-four years old.

The funeral took place on a cold, gray day. Mrs.

Shew supplied a fine linen dress for Virginia to be buried in, but Poe was not so fortunate in his apparel; he had only his old West Point overcoat to wrap tightly around himself as protection against the wind. Only days before, it had covered Virginia. At the last moment someone remembered to do a picture of Virginia. It was a haunting, chilling watercolor sketch of Poe's child-wife, in death. Later it was retouched to portray the dead girl's eyes as open.

As she was lowered into the grave, Poe must have realized at last that, save for Mrs. Clemm, he was alone in the world. He returned to the cottage, accompanied by Mrs. Clemm and Mrs. Shew, in a state of near-total collapse. The sufferings of the unhappy Virginia were over. But in the gloomy, tortured life of Edgar Poe there was still one more act to be played.

# 7

## *closing stanzas*
## (1847–1849)

In the winter of 1846–47, while Virginia Poe was gasping for breath in her tiny cubbyhole bedroom at Fordham, General Zachary Scott—"Old Rough and Ready"—was spurring fast-moving columns of American soldiers into the heartland of Mexico. A few congressmen from Northern states protested, claiming that President James K. Polk had maneuvered the United States into a war. It was, they charged, a war of aggression intended to add new territories suitable for the expansion of the South's cotton-slave economy. One of the protesting lawmakers, a little known congressman from Illinois named Abraham Lincoln, challenged Polk to name the "spot" where, according to the president, "American blood was shed on American soil." As thanks for his concern, Lincoln's constituents refused to reelect him.

They, like much of the nation, believed that it was America's "Manifest Destiny"—its inevitable fate—to spread the blessings of democracy to the entire continent, perhaps even to the entire Western hemisphere and beyond. Barely was the ink dry in 1848 on the peace treaty ending the Mexican-American War when gold was discovered in California. The lure of easy riches touched off a frenzied exodus of greedy prospectors from the cities of the settled eastern seaboard, across the Great Plains or around Cape Horn to the gold fields and the lawless boom towns of the Pacific coast.

The nation's feverish quest for gold and new territories held little interest for Edgar Allan Poe. Desolate with grief, his jangled nerves in near-total collapse, Poe was reduced for a time to almost complete dependence on Mrs. Clemm. He could not bear to be alone at night, and she would often sit by his bedside into the early morning hours, holding his hand, before he would drop off to sleep. At other times he would stumble his way to the cemetery and there, alone in the night, weep uncontrollably at the grave of his lost love.

In 1848, the year following Virginia's death, Poe produced two significant works: the poem "Ulalume" and the long prose poem *Eureka*. In "Ulalume" he returns with Psyche (his mind) to a strange and eerie landscape:

> And we passed to the end of the vista,
> But were stopped by the door of a tomb—

For the melancholy Poe only one outcome can be expected:

'Tis the vault of thy lost Ulalume!

The poet has returned to the place "On *this* very night of last year . . . that I brought a dead burden down here." The setting, like the misty lowlands of Poe's youth in Scotland, is fraught with romance, and sentiment, and dread loneliness:

Well I know, now, this dim lake of Auber—
This misty mid region of Weir—
Well I know, now, this dank tarn of Auber,
This ghoul-haunted woodland of Weir.

In *Eureka*, by contrast, Poe displays his intellect and rationality, perhaps at a time when he feared greatly for his sanity. *Eureka* required nearly two and a half hours to read aloud, although Poe always had argued that to maintain audience interest no poem should take longer than half an hour to recite. Poe was attempting to explain in lyrical terms in *Eureka* his scientific view of the universe. All created things, he said, spring from Nothingness and eventually return to Nothingness; therefore the Unity of all matter will come when matter disappears. To arrive at his proof, Poe digested (or half digested) the dominant scientific theories of his day. This took prodigious reading over many years, as well as the imagination and skill to express philosophical concepts in poetic language. It was his major effort to explain existence and death.

To him, *Eureka* was a deeply felt synthesis of all that he had learned. The public response, however, was little more than a disappointed yawn; they customarily looked to Poe for entertainment, not philosophy. And *Eureka* was by no measure as catchy as "The Raven."

The despondent Poe, meanwhile, occupied himself mostly with the simple pursuits of country life. He spent his days gardening and walking in the country with "Muddie," trying to regain his health and mental equilibrium. Sometimes he talked with a friendly priest in the nearby Catholic college at Fordham.

But as always he looked for a harbor of tranquility in the company of a woman. This time it was Mrs. Marie Louise Shew, who in Virginia's final days had ministered to the dying girl with such kindness. Mrs. Shew, an experienced nurse with social connections among New York's most respected physicians, considered Poe's physical symptoms to be serious—a combination of heart disease and a possible brain tumor. Without actually examining Poe, her medical friends tended to confirm her diagnosis. She brought him food and clothing. As might have been expected, Poe fell in love with her and became hopelessly dependent on her.

Once, when he was unable to concentrate on his writing, she is said to have brought him pen and paper. She then suggested that he write a poem on the sound of bells, a theme he had been considering. Poe began to write. Eventually "The Bells," with its manic throbbing, became, next to "The Raven," his most popular poem. There is a steady increase in the wild tempo of the piece from the delightfully gentle first stanza which speaks of "the tintinnabulation that so musically wells/ . . . From the jingling and the tinkling of the bells." In the final stanza even the maddening, swelling clangor gives way to hopelessness and death:

> To the tolling of the bells,
> Of the bells, bells, bells, bells—
> Bells, bells, bells—
> To the moaning and the groaning of the bells.

Responding to Mrs. Shew's sympathy and care, Poe recovered at least partially from the exhaustion that had brought him to the brink of death. But Mrs. Shew was a person of considerable common sense, as well as social position. She had no intention of being drawn into a complex personal relationship with the erratic poet for whom she had done so much. Gossip concerning Poe had already damaged the reputation of Frances Osgood. Instead Mrs. Shew urged him to seek a more permanent domestic arrangement—marriage to a woman who could give him the continuing care that he needed.

Depressed over the loss of Mrs. Shew, Poe nevertheless saw the logic in her advice. He set out to find a wife. But while he looked he became even more dependent on Mrs. Clemm. By now she was truly not his aunt or mother-in-law, but in fact as the term "Muddie" suggested, his mother. It was for her that he wrote the moving poem, "To My Mother," with its famous lines:

> My mother—my own mother, who died early,
>     Was but the mother of myself; but you
> Are mother to the one I loved so dearly,
>     And thus are dearer than the mother I
>     knew. . . .

The next of Poe's romantic interests was Mrs. Sarah Helen Whitman, the vision Poe had first beheld at a distance in a rose garden. Seldom in literary history has there been a stranger romance. Mrs. Whitman was a well-to-do widow who lived in Providence, Rhode Island. She was also a "spiritualist," fascinated by the occult and the mysterious, given to holding seances in semidarkened rooms to convene the spirits of the departed. She enjoyed dressing dramatically in long, flowing robes, and drawing all eyes to herself when she entered a room. It is said that she often carried a handkerchief drenched in chloroform to dull her senses. Mrs. Whitman also produced streams of sickeningly sentimental poetry, which was the occasion for her initial contact with Edgar Poe.

At her Valentine's Day party in February 1848, Mrs. Whitman read a poem to "The Raven," praising Poe and suggesting that if he were her love

> Not a bird that roams the forest
> Shall our lofty eyrie share

At that point the two had never met. Poe learned of the poem through Mrs. Osgood and immediately began to plan some excuse to visit Mrs. Whitman's home.

Before he could arrange the trip he lectured on "The Poetic Principle" at Lowell, Massachusetts. There he met Mrs. Annie Richmond and, spellbound by what he called the "unworldliness" of her "deep-set eyes," at once became infatuated with her. As he declared in a letter describing his first meeting with Annie, "I know not how it is, but this peculiar expression of the eye, wreathing itself occasionally into the lips, is the most powerful, if not absolutely the sole spell which rivets my interest in woman."* Unfortunately for him, Mrs. Richmond already had a husband.

*Allen, *Israfel*, pp. 608–09.

Confused, but now determined to become rich in any possible way, Poe hurriedly left for Richmond, Virginia, to find financial backing for *The Stylus,* which he still talked vaguely about operating some day. Scarcely had he arrived in his former hometown than he went on a drinking spree that lasted two weeks. Finally friends from the *Southern Literary Messenger* heard of his plight. They located him in a saloon on the Richmond waterfront and brought him to the home of the Mackenzies, where his sister Rosalie was still living. There he recovered.

Poe remained in Richmond less than two months. He spent most of his time visiting old friends, reciting his poetry, and doing minor writing chores at the *Messenger.* Once he rashly challenged John Daniel, the editor of another journal, to a duel—Daniel having accused Poe of pursuing Mrs. Whitman only for her property. Daniel invited Poe to his office, and pointing calmly to a pair of old dueling pistols on the desk offered to settle the argument then and there. Poe, although rash and erratic, was by no means a fool. He made light of the matter, and by the end of the interview had convinced Daniel to accompany him across the street to a tavern for some good cheer instead of a blood bath.

Returning to Fordham in September 1848, Poe wasted no time before arranging a meeting with

Mrs. Whitman in Providence. When at last they met, characteristically (for both) in a graveyard, Poe proposed marriage at once. A torrid correspondence began—love letters written by two imaginative people who reveled in the use of words to express romantic affection. Even for a sentimental age, Edgar Poe and Helen Whitman were master practitioners of the art of sickishly sweet love notes; Poe, of course, usually put his literary talents to other purposes.

Mrs. Whitman would not give Poe a definite answer to his proposal. She was concerned with the gossip about his previous dealings with women; her family was convinced that the untrustworthy Poe had his eyes on her property. Poe chose to wait for Mrs. Whitman's answer in Lowell, Massachusetts, near Annie Richmond. His passion for Mrs. Richmond grew greater by the day, as did his confusion and despair.

In early November he left for Providence, but not before winning a promise from Annie that in the event of his illness she would visit him and let him die in her arms. He was willing to do almost anything to see her again—even face death. By now Poe was too restless to stay in one place long enough to do serious writing; he gave himself up to frantic activity, often in the form of travel. In Boston he bought two ounces of the opiate laudanum, and drank an overdose of it. Instead of killing him the drug triggered a fit of severe vomiting. Thoroughly sick and exhausted, Poe proceeded on by train to Providence.

By November 14 he had persuaded Mrs. Whitman to marry him. But, probably at the urging of her relatives, she insisted on two conditions: that Poe not have access to her estate; and that he never again use alcohol. With considerable resentment Poe agreed to the humiliating conditions. Then, still weak from his bout with laudanum, he returned to "Muddie" at the Fordham cottage.

Poe wrote once more to Annie, proposing that she leave her husband and marry him. But she wanted no part of the match. So, returning to Providence, Poe completed the arrangements for his marriage to Mrs. Whitman. By now his mind was deeply agitated by the complicated romantic entanglement in which he found himself.

On December 23, 1848, two days before the wedding was to have taken place, Helen Whitman broke the engagement. She had been told by friends that on that very day Poe had been seen drinking wine with friends at a hotel bar. He denied it, but Helen, although lost in tears, firmly insisted that she would not marry him.

Poe's pride was deeply scarred. But he was also relieved at his escape from a marriage to his "second choice." He returned home alone to the astonished Mrs. Clemm.

For a time Poe found comfort in his writings. He suffered now from incessant headaches. Still he managed to produce one of his most beautiful poems, "Annabel Lee," again using the theme of a love for a lost bride, a love which endures even beyond the grave. "Eldorado," also written at this time, concludes that true happiness comes not in gold but only in death.

Death, always close to the forefront of Poe's mind, must have seemed especially near in the winter of 1848–49. Although his work was in demand by magazines and newspapers, exhaustion slowed his writing pace; the headaches became more painful. Yet he never completely stopped writing.

In April 1849, Poe received a letter from E. H. N. Patterson of Oquawka, Illinois. Patterson offered financial backing for *The Stylus*. It appears that he had long admired Poe's works and when he came into an inheritance, leaped at the opportunity to collaborate with the illustrious Eastern author.

Poe replied with enthusiasm and eventually obtained a fifty dollar advance toward expenses from Patterson for a trip to Richmond; there he hoped to gather subscriptions for the long dreamed of magazine.

Before leaving he arranged with his former enemy Rufus Griswold for a compilation of his complete works and also appointed Griswold literary executor in case of his death. He left "Muddie" in the care of Mrs. S. A. Lewis, a wealthy poet who had replaced Marie Louise Shew as the dispenser of kindnesses to the unhappy writer and his mother-in-law.

On June 29 Poe said a warm farewell to Mrs. Clemm, promising to "be good" while he was away and to come back "to love and comfort you." But he told Mrs. Lewis of a premonition that he would never return.

Little is known about what happened next, except that while waiting to change trains in Philadelphia he decided to take a drink in a saloon. Several days later he appeared at the offices of *Sartain's Magazine*. Delirious and trembling he begged for protection against imaginary conspirators who, he said, were following him and trying to kill him. He asked Sartain to shave off his moustache to disguise his appearance. He also told of spending a night in prison for intoxication until he was recognized and freed.

Poe pleaded for laudanum, but Sartain and two other friends cared for him with good food until he was well enough to travel. Then they bought him a train ticket to Richmond and saw him on his way.

He arrived in the city of his boyhood deathly sick, his clothing in horrible condition, and deeply ashamed of his weakness along the route. But his sister Rosalie and her foster parents, the Mackenzies, nursed him to recovery, and in a few days he was well enough to visit old friends.

By now Poe was a literary celebrity in Richmond. As he walked in the streets little boys rushed up to ask for his autograph; the city's scholars sought him out for discussion; he was welcomed into the homes of his childhood friends.

The true purpose of his visit to Richmond was probably less the gathering of subscriptions for *The Stylus* than the completion of a marriage arrangement. He hoped to persuade Elmira Royster Shelton—the "Lost Lenore" of his youth and now a comfortably situated widow—to marry him. He and Mrs. Clemm had concluded that in his poor health it was only through such a secure marriage that he could survive. His weak heart could no longer stand the strain of financial uncertainty or the stimulants that doctors had warned him would be fatal if he continued to use them.

Poe began a whirlwind courtship. He touched on every chord of Elmira's memory, reminding her especially of how her parents had intercepted his letters and then maneuvered her into a marriage she did not really want. He walked with her to places they had shared as young lovers. Since she had become religiously devout he even went to church with her—a major concession considering his distaste for organized religion. He joined the local branch of the Sons of Temperance and seems to have been reasonably successful in staying away from drink. His lectures and poetry recitations in Richmond and Norfolk were well received. At last he was respected and admired in his own home country.

Eight days before the end of September 1849, Elmira Shelton agreed to marry Poe. The wedding date was set for October 17.

Elmira wrote a warm, loving note to Mrs. Clemm, introducing herself and graciously setting the tone for their future relationship. Edgar was to return briefly to the cottage at Fordham to bring "Muddie" to Richmond for the wedding. Then she would remain in the Southern city, making her home with the newlyweds.

Perhaps, after all, the story would have a happy ending.

Poe spent September 26 paying courtesy calls on good friends before leaving for the North. One call was at the office of Dr. W. Gibbon Carter, a long-time adviser and companion. Before leaving he borrowed Dr. Carter's finely wrought Malacca cane.

Then Poe dined happily with a congenial party of Richmond cronies. They stayed with him until four o'clock in the morning when his boat was to leave for Baltimore, a stopping-off point on the way to New York. He was in a state of excitement about his coming marriage, but did not take a drink. The men all accompanied him to the dock. Then they waved goodbye and turned to pick their way through the deserted streets, as the steamboat pulled off into the early morning Nothingness.

It was less than a week later that Joseph Walker, typesetter for the *Baltimore Sun,* was hurrying along busy Lombard Street in Baltimore on election day in that city. The disheveled figure sprawled in the gutter outside of Gunner's Hall tavern at first did not catch his attention. But the handsome Malacca cane clutched in the poor unfortunate's hand did.

The rest is history.

# epilogue

Edgar Allan Poe was buried on October 9, 1849, in the cemetery of Westminster Presbyterian Church in Baltimore. Mrs. Clemm moved from the home of first one of Poe's "flames" to another, dogged always by poverty and unhappiness. She survived the Civil War and finally died in 1871 at a church home for the aged in Baltimore. She was laid to rest beside the remains of Edgar.

In 1875 the trio that once had strolled together along the flowered country lanes of Fordham finally was reunited. The cemetery where Virginia Poe had lain since 1847 was needed for new construction. When it was destroyed a Poe biographer removed Virginia's bones and, after keeping them in a box under his bed for a time, arranged for their reburial alongside the bodies of "Sissy's" beloved mother and husband. Rosalie Mackenzie Poe was forced out of Richmond by the Civil War and died in a home for the aged in 1874.

Poe was scarcely cold in his grave when a storm

of literary controversy burst around his memory. A scurrilous obituary in the *New York Tribune* written by Rufus Griswold set the tone of the attacks that followed. Griswold continued to malign Poe's reputation and character in a vitriolic account of his subject's life appended to the "collected works," which Poe naively had entrusted for editing to his jealous rival. Griswold went so far as to destroy important correspondence and even to change some of Poe's own writings.

Appalled by Griswold's skullduggery, Poe's admirers rushed to his defense. In the forefront of his champions was Mrs. Sarah Helen Whitman, who had come to idealize her romantic relationship with the poet. Before long a whole host of detractors and a few loyal defenders entered the battle, until it became next to impossible to uncover the truth.

As a result there soon grew up around Poe a dark legend. He was the mysterious, brooding poet, wailing to the dead at midnight in windswept graveyards, his black Spanish cape wrapped tightly about him, his piercing eyes staring morbidly from beneath the well known high forehead. This mixture was in turn compounded with stories of his drinking, his resort to opium, his sexual excesses or inadequacies, his untrustworthiness with money, his charlatanism.

According to Baudelaire, Poe was trapped and driven to insanity by America, "a great barbarous realm equipped with gas fixtures." Unquestionably Poe was out of place in a land where success was measured in accumulated wealth and physical endurance. He had neither. But it is probably true, too, that for Poe there could not have been much greater happiness in *any* human society. His vision was so unusual, so peculiar, that to the comfortably mediocre he would always have posed a threat.

Ultrasensitive, a poet and dreamer, he was thrown unprepared into the harsh realities of everyday existence. Increasingly he withdrew into himself, obsessed with his own problems. The literary introspection and pride of his youthful days were exaggerated many times over. In his later essays he very nearly proclaimed superiority to all living beings and a kinship with God; this self-adulation was paralleled, however, with a growing sense of inferiority and personal misery. But always the focus was on himself. When, through his stories, he laughed, he laughed with contempt at the rest of mankind. When he mourned his "dead ladies" he mourned for himself, not for the human predicament.

Yet Poe endures. His works are eagerly reproduced; interest in his personality continues high. Perhaps after all there is something perennially enticing about his ghoulish creations, something electrically alive about the characters he conjured in the "haunted palace" of his mind. Generation after generation of new readers have become fascinated by the terrifying dream world fashioned by his imagination. We know revulsion for the horrors he portrays, but at the same time are attracted by the originality of the amoral kingdom he opens before us.

Others have tried to imitate him—to capture in poetry and the short story the effect of grotesque horror which was his hallmark. But none have ever completely succeeded in scaling the walls of the lonely fortress that Poe built for himself through his work. He was unique. And it is in Poe's awesome uniqueness that he finds his niche in literature. It was his burden. It was also the source of his tormented genius.

# bibliography

Poe's interest to literary scholars has extended beyond his few superb stories and exquisitely wrought lyric poems; studies of even his minor works are voluminous. He has also been an irresistible subject for biographers, some attracted mainly by the more lurid aspects of his turbulent career.

The most enjoyable and rewarding way to approach Poe is to read his works directly. A readily available and inexpensive source is *The Complete Tales and Poems of Edgar Allan Poe,* Modern Library (New York: Random House, 1938), edited by Hervey Allen. See also *The Complete Poems and Stories of Edgar Allan Poe, with Selections from his Critical Writings,* edited by Arthur Hobson Quinn and Edward H. O'Neill, 2 volumes (New York: Knopf, 1946).

The biography of Poe generally considered most reliable—and certainly the most comprehensive—is Arthur Hobson Quinn's massive *Edgar*

*Allan Poe: A Critical Biography* (New York: Appleton-Century-Crofts, 1941). Also scholarly, but more interestingly written than Quinn's portrayal is Hervey Allan's *Israfel: The Life and Times of Edgar Allan Poe* (New York: Farrar and Rinehart, 1934), a source whose insights the present author gratefully acknowledges.

Edward Wagenknecht has prepared a searching study with important critical and psychological observations: *Edgar Allan Poe: The Man Behind the Legend* (New York: Oxford University Press, 1963). For stimulating, exceptionally well written critical look at Poe's works, see Daniel Hoffman's *Poe, Poe, Poe, Poe, Poe, Poe, Poe* (New York: Doubleday Anchor, 1973).

# some important dates in the life of edgar allan poe

| | |
|---|---|
| 1809 | Edgar Poe born in Boston, January 19. |
| 1810 | Elizabeth Arnold Poe, deserted by her husband, David, moves to Richmond with her three young children. |
| 1811 | On death of Elizabeth Poe (December 8) Edgar is taken into the household of John Allan, a Richmond merchant, but not formally adopted. Now called Edgar Allan Poe. |
| 1815–20 | Edgar accompanies the Allans to England. Attends the Manor House School at Stoke Newington and other schools. |
| 1820–25 | Edgar's boyhood in Richmond. Reads widely and begins first attempts at poetry. Develops idealistic love for Jane Stith Stanard ("Helen"), who dies in 1824. |
| 1826 | Informally engaged to Sarah Elmira Royster. |

| 1826 | Enrolls at University of Virginia (February) but returns to Richmond (December), having contracted sizeable gambling debts which John Allan refuses to pay. Sarah Elmira Royster becomes engaged to another man. |
| 1827 | Edgar leaves John Allan's home after serious quarrel. Publishes *Tamerlane and Other Poems*. Enlisted in United States Army under alias Edgar A. Perry. |
| 1829 | Temporary reconciliation between Poe and Allan after death of Mrs. Allan. Poe leaves the army. |
| 1830 | Enters West Point to please Allan. |
| 1831 | Unsuccessful in gaining financial support from Allan, Poe intentionally disobeys orders and is dismissed from West Point. Lives first in New York and then in Baltimore household of his aunt, Mrs. Maria Clemm, and cousin, Virginia. |
| 1832 | Poe's attempt at reconciliation with Allan fails. Publishes five stories. |
| 1833 | Wins fifty-dollar prize for "MS. Found in a Bottle." |
| 1834 | Death of John Allan. Poe receives no legacy. |
| 1835 | Becomes assistant to Thomas W. White of *Southern Literary Messenger* |

in Richmond. Secretly marries his cousin Virginia.

1836     A second, public, marriage ceremony with Virginia; she was thirteen at the time.

1837     Leaves *Southern Literary Messenger,* hoping for success and recognition in New York.

1838     Publishes *The Narrative of Arthur Gordon Pym.* Moves to Philadelphia.

1839     Becomes editor of *Burton's Gentleman's Magazine. Tales of the Grotesque and Arabesque.*

1841     Agrees to edit *Graham's Magazine.*

1842     Poe leaves *Graham's Magazine.* Becomes aware of Virginia's serious illness. His drinking increases.

1843–44     Poe struggles to found own magazine but fails. Ekes out bare living as freelance journalist before moving to New York. Becomes editor of N. P. Willis's *New York Evening Mirror.*

1845     Poe publishes "The Raven" and becomes famous overnight.

1845–46     Joins the *Broadway Journal* with one-third share in magazine's operation. Eventually becomes editor and proprietor.

1846     Abandons the *Broadway Journal* and, as Virginia's health continues to deteriorate, takes up secluded life at Fordham, on outskirts of New York City.

1847    Death of Virginia (January 30). Poe experiences physical and mental collapse but is aided by Marie Louise Shew.

1848    Poe seeks refuge in feminine companionship with series of doting admirers. Concludes marriage agreement with Mrs. Sarah Helen Whitman but she breaks engagement on suspicion that he has lapsed from pledge not to drink. Writes "The Bells," "Eldorado," and *Eureka*.

1849    Writes "Annabel Lee." Returns to Richmond and becomes engaged to Sarah Elmira Royster, sweetheart of his youth, now widowed. On stopover at Baltimore under circumstances never completely clear, becomes ill and, after great mental agony, dies (October 7, 1849).

# index